EARTHSHIP

SYSTEMS AND COMPONENTS

Michael E. Reynolds

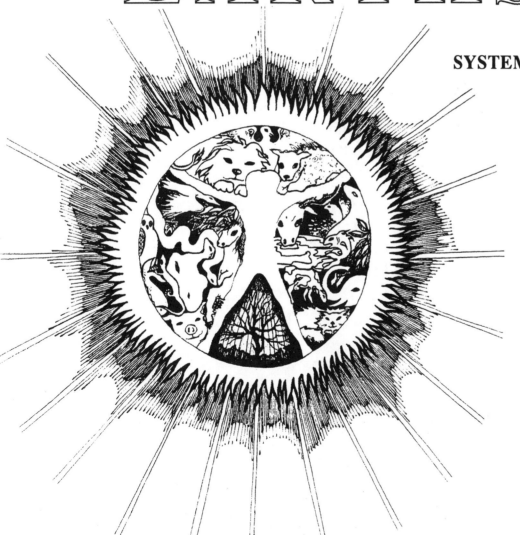

SOLAR SURVIVAL ARCHITECTURE
P.O. Box 1041
Taos, New Mexico 87571
EARTH

Special Thanks to

Gerry and Dennis Weaver
    for continuing to pursue the evolution of the Earthship concept.

Claire Blanchard and Pam Freund
    for helping to put this book together.

Duane Davis, Ken Anderson, Peter Lusk
    for their contributions to the book.

Joe Hoar
    for help in evolving Earthship systems.

Catherine Hale and Karlis Visceps
    for sharing catch water experience.

**Pam Freund, Jonah Reynolds, Justin Simpson, Peter Kolshorn, Duane Davis
Chris Simpson, Peter Wilson and Bill Acheff**
    for photography.

John Hunt and Glenn Sweet
    for helping to evolve the gravity skylight.

Front cover photo - **Pam Freund**
Back cover photo - **Bill Acheff**

My wife Chris...

CONTENTS

THEY LANDED IN HUGE VESSELS AND SLOWLY WALKED OUT ONTO THE LAND. THEY DESTROYED EVERY HUMAN IN THEIR PATH. THEY MOVED INTO THE CITIES. SYSTEMATICALLY AND DELIBERATELY, THEY SOUGHT OUT AND CONSUMED MEN, WOMEN AND CHILDREN. NOTHING COULD STOP THEM.

THE ABOVE PARAGRAPH SOUNDS LIKE A TYPICAL SPACE INVADERS MOVIE IN WHICH WE HAVE PORTRAYED THE SPACE INVADERS AS THE RUTHLESS ENEMY. THE FOLLOWING STORY PUTS THIS PARAGRAPH IN A DIFFERENT CONTEXT DERIVED FROM A BROADER THAN HUMAN VIEW. PERHAPS WE SHOULD LOOK AT OURSELVES THIS WAY AS WE DETERMINE JUST WHO THE ENEMY IS AND WHETHER OR NOT WE HAVE A FUTURE.

The beings from Alcyone traveled as thoughts. This is much faster than the speed of light. It is instantaneous. Light speed has limits - significant limits relative to the size of our universe. For instance, the closest star to the Earth is thousands of light years away. What good is light speed in a universe of these dimensions? Thoughts, on the other hand, travel instantaneously. There is no need for cumbersome bodies in the world of thoughts. Thoughts are energy and energy travels and penetrates any material barrier anywhere, anytime - instantaneously. Think about it - if you think of the house where you grew up or your room when you were ten years old, how long does it take your mind to take you there? This is how the beings from Alcyone traveled. When many were going to the same place, they traveled as one thought - a phenomenon we have only talked and written about here on Earth. Can you imagine the power and focus of many with the same thought?

It is easy to think about someplace you've been and to allow your thoughts to take you there. The real masters of thought travel can explore places *they haven't been before.* This opens the whole universe to exploration. This is what the beings from Alcyone were doing. They were exploring the universe with much the same ignorance and innocence that we are currently (in the twentieth century - Earth) exploring our solar system.

The incidents that are documented in the following pages describe what they found and how they reacted to what they saw.

A group of three beings had merged into one thought and were cruising in a spiral galaxy. They drifted into a solar system that had what appeared to be nine or ten planets orbiting around one sun. The sun was a fairly stable main sequence star. They observed different phenomena and beings on the different planets. On the third planet out from the sun there existed a beauty the three beings had never imagined or seen before in their travels of the universe. There was such a delicate balance and harmony of intertwined existence that the whole planet seemed to be a single living creature.

In the world of the three beings from Alcyone, time was not much of a factor. They watched and observed the planet for thousands of Earth years and actually grew to love it and visit it as often as one would visit a friend. They saw the waters running and talking. They saw the trees dancing and laughing. They saw the animals participating in one overall pulse of existence that was woven like a tapestry throughout the planet. The three Alcyonites were very careful not to interrupt the slightest feather of this existence as they recognized the beauty of the balance.

At some point in their observations of this planet they began to see the emergence of another creature. This creature was very similar to some of the animal creatures on this planet but it was different. The invisible threads that wove the animals to the planet did not exist for these new creatures. They were not part of the tapestry. They were aliens to this beautiful world. They came from somewhere else. They were invaders. The Alcyonites watched ever growing numbers of these tiny parasites attack their friend. *Imagine watching a good friend attacked and eaten by thousands of carnivorous ants.*

The Alcyonites were very alarmed and began to study their friend, the blue/green planet, much more closely. They watched these new creatures cut the green trees - at first just a few - then, as the creatures prolifically multiplied, serious numbers of trees disappeared from the planet leaving huge bald scars on the mountains. They watched the slaughter of animals of every kind, again, just a few at first then progressing until many animal species were totally wiped out. This new creature seemed to consume or destroy all other life on the planet. It also produced some of the most awful, knarlly substances the Alcyonites had ever seen. Much of the beauty and life of their friend was being destroyed. Not only were the new creatures destroying the animals, plants and, consequently, the balance and pulse of the planet itself, they were also trying to destroy each other, bringing about even more devastation in the process. To the Alcyonites, these new creatures appeared to be the most hostile, aggressive and ruthless beings they had ever observed in the universe. They found themselves just watching while their friend was being consumed by these hostile new creatures. Their friend, the blue/green planet, was very strong and enduring but these new creatures were multiplying very rapidly. The Alcyonites began to see the obvious - *their friend, if it survived, was already losing something in this process that it might never regain.* The Alcyonites began to wonder - Do these new creatures have the right to do this? Do they have the right to take the beautiful blue/green away from this planet?

The Alcyonites returned to their galaxy and reported what they had seen to an intergalactic "committee" of ancient and wise beings. They decided (based on broad observation) that the new creatures which had appeared on the blue/green planet in the spiral galaxy were, in fact, a hostile, aggressive, galactic virus which should be destroyed before it spread to other planets and galaxies. A small band of destroyers was sent to the planet to wipe out the hostile virus. They left as a single thought and upon arrival they manifest into the very fears and elemental hallucinations of the virus itself...

THEY LANDED IN HUGE VESSELS AND SLOWLY WALKED OUT ONTO THE LAND. THEY DESTROYED EVERY HUMAN IN THEIR PATH. THEY MOVED INTO THE CITIES. SYSTEMATICALLY AND DELIBERATELY, THEY SOUGHT OUT AND CONSUMED MEN, WOMEN AND CHILDREN. NOTHING COULD STOP THEM.

Following photos: Distant views of the REACH community.

INTRODUCTION

This volume of the EARTHSHIP series will deal mostly with systems and components of the vessel. With regard to these systems and components, we must realize that we, the users of the vessel, are part of the vessel. This is much the same as we, the users of the Earth, are part of the Earth.

When children play jump rope, the rope is turned by two children, one at each end. The child who is going to jump stands beside the turning rope and begins to move with the motion of the rope to align herself with the rhythm before she jumps in. It doesn't take a child long to learn that the rhythm of the rope prevails if you want to be good at jump rope. The child learns that it must become part of the system.

When you are pushing someone in a swing, you don't just push them whenever you want to, you wait until they swing all the way back and gravity is just about to take them back the other way. You join with gravity to give them an extra boost in the direction that gravity was already pulling them. Your push aligns with the pendulum motion of the swing. You apply your force as an integral part of the system.

In both of these examples the existing system prevailed without challenge and the person became part of the system in order to benefit from it. This is much the same way a chameleon takes on the surrounding colors to hide from predators. This is the posture of the EARTHSHIP and all its systems. **The EARTHSHIP is a participant in the prevailing systems of the planet Earth. It causes no conflict, no stress, no depletion, no trauma.**

For us to live in EARTHSHIPS is as simple as a child stepping in to a turning jump rope. The child was a "chameleon" - it adopted the rhythm of the rope. Can we adopt the rhythms of the planet? This is our dilemma. We are unwilling or unable to drop our preconceived, arbitrary, "synthetic" rhythms for those of the planet. This is like the child trying to get the rope to adapt to her rhythm or a chameleon trying to get a leaf to change to it's color. **The chameleon who waits for the leaf to change colors will get eaten.** We are making synthetic energy, burning fossil fuels and ruining natural balances trying to get the *leaf to change to our color*. It would be much easier and more healthy for us and for the planet if we changed ourselves to the color of the leaf. Our "synthetic rhythms" are born out of our socioeconomic structure which is based on dogmatic religions, corrupted politics, hollow economics, fear, greed and basic lust for power. There is a lot of "gravity" in this socioeconomic structure that demands so much of us. An over view of this structure could very well *make us look like the enemy*. This and the fact that our socioeconomic structure is obviously flailing should make us look to the "rhythm of the rope" - "the color of the leaves" - the patterns of the planet. If we can step into the "rhythm of the rope", we can cruise free and comfortable in EARTHSHIPS for thousands of years to come.

We definitely need comfortable temperatures, light, electricity, hot water, food, sewage treatment, etc. These necessities are all available within the framework of a certain "rhythm" in the EARTHSHIP concept. The more we are able to align our priorities and needs with the prevailing rhythms of the planet, the easier and less expensive (both in terms of economics and ecology) they will be to obtain.

Some basic examples of this alignment present the following questions:

Do you need to do a wash whenever you want to or can you exist only doing washes on sunny days?

Do you need limitless hot water all the time or can you survive using hot water between 11 a.m. and 11 p.m. on sunny days?

Do you need three square meals of meat and potatoes each day or can you graze from a year - round greenhouse?

Do you need limitless electricity for hundreds of plastic gadgets or can you exist with a small amount of electricity for a few special tools and appliances?

Do you need hot water instantly at your tap or can you wait a few seconds for it to get there?

Do you need three showers a day or can you survive on one every other day with sponge baths between?

Do you need to flush away five gallons of water every time you use a toilet or can you use a compost toilet?

Do you need to keep your house at 78 degrees all the time or can the temperature drop to 68 degrees some times?

Do you need five-hundred gallons of water every day or can you exist with 20 gallons some days?

If our lifestyles can conform more to the patterns of the planet than to our socioeconomic system, we can reduce the stress on both ourselves and the planet. This is easier said than done due to the "reality" and the "gravity" of mortgage payments, utility bills and the generally high cost of eating and living. Most of us have no choice. We have to be places at certain times looking certain ways in order to make the money needed to make those payments. However, many people have built EARTHSHIPS themselves and ended up with little or no mortgage payment. They also have little or no utility bills and their ability to grow food year-round inside the EARTHSHIP has greatly effected what they have to spend on packaged, processed foods. *This is approaching the freedom this country was founded on.* I do not think we are a hostile, aggressive virus on this planet. We have simply built a trap and now we are caught in it. Our efforts to survive in this trap make us appear ruthless, hostile and aggressive. The EARTHSHIP and the EARTHSHIP concepts can begin to free us from this trap. Then we will have the mental space to make choices. As it is, most of us have no choice. **When the wolf is at your door, there is little time to think of anything but survival.**

Freedom from our trap is as available as the bus that you catch down on the corner. You must make the small journey - *take the small step* - to go down to the corner to catch the bus. The same is true for aligning with (catching) the rhythms of the planet. We have to take the small journey to a *position* where we can align with natural phenomena. The journey to the bus-stop is on foot. The journey to alignment with natural phenomena is in our minds. To go to the bus-stop, you must walk outside your living room, on to the street and down to the corner. *Then you simply ride the bus.* To get to the "EARTHSHIP-stop" you must walk <u>outside your dogma,</u> on to the Earth and into its natural patterns. *Then you simply ride the Earth.*
The exit from our dogma (the trap we have created) is guarded by a dragon. This dragon is not just a dream, it is very real. Some say our reality is just a reflection of our dreams and vice-versa. Dream therapists say that you are everyone in your dream. If a dragon is chasing you in your dream, you are both yourself and the dragon. The dragon is an aspect of your psyche. Dreams show us that one aspect of ourselves can create problems for another, i.e. **we** are our own worst enemies. **We are the dragon that is guarding our exit from dogma.**

I had a dream that I was an angel. I knew how to fly. While cruising around, high in the sky, I saw flames coming out of a cave in the ground. I glided down closer and saw a dragon come out of the flaming cave. He followed a riverbed down to a small town and I watched him begin devastating the town. Then he looked up and saw me flying. I could see his orange eyes, with the thin vertical black slit for a pupil, looking up at me. He began communicating with me telepathically. I was amazed. He wanted to learn how to fly. Thinking fast, I agreed to teach him to fly if he would quit devastating the town. Apparently flying was more interesting to him than devastating the town so he agreed. I taught him to fly and the last thing I remember was flying beside him looking over into his orange eyes and seeing a happiness in those once angry, violent, orange eyes.

According to dream therapists, I was both myself and the dragon. I was both the devastator and the teacher. We, as a society, are, in fact, both our devastators and our teachers. Half of the distance we must go to learn to live in peace and harmony with the Earth (and each other) must be traveled in our own minds, between ourselves and our dragons. *We must teach them to fly.* There is definitely a part of us that simply wants to consume, however, like the dragon in my dream, maybe flying would be more interesting. The EARTHSHIP concept explained in Volume One greatly reduces the emphasis on consumption and proposes alignment with limitless natural phenomena. This results in a freedom not unlike flying when compared to the restrictions placed on the average dependent consumer in today's society.

If you want to fly, you must learn about riding *on* the wind - not harnessing the wind - not capturing the wind, but *riding the wind.* If we want to sail on the seas of tomorrow, we must learn about *riding* the Earth - not harnessing the Earth - not capturing or exploiting the Earth, but *riding the Earth.* Astronauts *ride* their space module. They have learned about its "rhythms" and they religiously relate to them lest they be stranded in space. They don't tear their space module apart making pieces to entertain themselves on their journey - they would be committing suicide if they did this. Buckminster Fuller was one of the first to call the Earth a space ship. Its rhythms are our only hope of survival. If we tear it apart to amuse ourselves on our journey, we are committing suicide. The systems and rhythms of a NASA space module evolved for the purpose of sustaining the lives of the astronauts. The astronauts themselves evolved through training relative to these systems. The same is true for our space module - the Earth. We were originally born out of its systems and rhythms and they will sustain us through millennia, not a big power plant with a big pile of plutonium. If the astronauts found themselves cold in their space module, would they gather up paper to build a fire on the floor? If they did, they would not be able to breathe then they would blow up. Does this sound familiar?

The Earth is our space module flying through space. We are riding it. The EARTHSHIP concepts serve as our operator's manual. We can self- destruct shortly after launch or we can sail into the future on the wings of universal energy patterns.

CAN YOU TOUCH THE GLOW OF MORNING AS IT DRIFTS INTO A DAY
CAN YOU BE THE MIGHTY MOUNTAIN WHEN YOU NEED TO BE THAT WAY
CAN YOU SEE THE GOD OF THUNDER AS HE ROLLS ACROSS THE SKY
CAN YOU SEE HE'S DROPPING FLOWER PETALS DOWN ON YOU AND I
CAN YOU FEEL THE REELING ENERGY FROM EVERY LIVING THING
CAN YOU SEE IT MAKES US HAPPY
CAN YOU SEE IT MAKES US SING

CAN YOU SEE INTO THE RAINBOW
CAN YOU SEE INTO THE WIND
CAN YOU SEE INTO THE STARLIGHT
CAN YOU SEE INTO YOUR FRIEND
CAN YOU YIELD INTO THE MOONLIGHT
CAN IT PENETRATE YOUR EYES
CAN YOU SEE IT MAKES US PEACEFUL
CAN YOU SEE IT MAKES US HIGH

CAN YOU PEEL AWAY YOUR DOGMA
CAN YOU PEEL AWAY YOUR FEAR
CAN YOU SEE YOUR JOURNEY'S ENDING
CAN YOU SEE IT STARTED HERE
CAN YOU PASS INTO THE SPIRIT
CAN YOU SEND IT WITH YOUR EYE
CAN YOU SEE IT MAKES US RISE UP
CAN YOU SEE IT MAKES US FLY

COME FLY WITH ME

PART ONE
SYSTEMS OF THE EARTHSHIP

*SOMETIMES IN NEW MEXICO WE GO UP INTO THE MOUNTAINS AND CUT STANDING DEAD TREES FOR OUR ROOF BEAMS. WE DRIVE THROUGH THE MOUNTAIN ROADS LOOKING FOR THEM. THEY ARE EASILY VISIBLE, AS THEY HAVE NO FOLIAGE. WHEN WE SPOT A STANDING DEAD, WE CUT IT, TRIM THE LIMBS OFF AND DRAG IT TO THE TRUCK. OFTEN, THESE ARE 18 TO 20 FOOT LONG LOGS ABOUT 12" IN DIAMETER. THEY ARE QUITE HEAVY AND IT USUALLY TAKES THREE OR FOUR PEOPLE AND/OR A WINCH WITH A HUNDRED FOOT CABLE TO DRAG THEM TO THE TRUCK. IN TERMS OF MONEY (IF YOU ARE PAYING THOSE WHO HELP YOU), THIS CAN GET EXPENSIVE. THERE WERE TIMES, BEFORE I HAD A WINCH, WHEN I DIDN'T REALLY HAVE THE MONEY TO HIRE HELP, AND I NEEDED LOGS. I WENT ANYWAY. I DROVE UP INTO THE MOUNTAINS AND FOUND SEVERAL STANDING DEAD TREES ON THE UPHILL SIDE OF THE MOUNTAIN ROAD. AS THE PRIMITIVE ROADS WERE CARVED OUT OF THE MOUNTAINSIDE, A VERTICAL CLIFF SOMETIMES TEN TO TWELVE FEET HIGH WAS FORMED. I BACKED MY TRUCK (WHICH HAD HEAVY DUTY RACKS), RIGHT UP INTO ONE OF THESE CLIFFS. UP THE MOUNTAIN SIDE I WENT WITH MY CHAIN SAW AND CUT SEVERAL STANDING DEAD TREES, TRIMMED THEM AND SIMPLY <u>GUIDED THEM DOWN THE MOUNTAIN.</u> I HAD A FRIEND WHO HELPED ME FOR FREE - **GRAVITY**. THERE ARE MANY FRIENDS LIKE GRAVITY WHO CAN HELP US <u>LIVE</u> FOR FREE. THEY WERE OUR DESIGN CONSULTANTS FOR THE EARTHSHIP, AND NOW THEY WILL BE OUR CONSULTANTS FOR THE <u>SYSTEMS OF THE EARTHSHIP</u>.*

1. SOLAR ELECTRIC
S Y S T E M S

THE OPERATION OF A SAILBOAT REQUIRES AN UNDERSTANDING OF THE CONCEPTS AND SCHEMATICS OF SAILING AND *KNOWING THE PATTERNS AND NATURE OF THE WIND*. THERE ARE MANY DIFFERENCES BETWEEN THE OPERATION OF A GASOLINE POWERED SPEED BOAT AND A WIND POWERED SAILBOAT. THE MAJOR DIFFERENCE IS THAT IN A SAILBOAT YOU WILL *NEVER RUN OUT OF GAS*. OTHER DIFFERENCES INVOLVE POLLUTION, NOISE, WEAR AND TEAR, AND REPAIR OF MOVING PARTS. THE DIFFERENCES BETWEEN CONVENTIONAL ELECTRICITY AND SOLAR ELECTRICITY IN A HOME ARE SIMILAR TO THE DIFFERENCES BETWEEN A SPEED BOAT AND A SAILBOAT.

THIS CHAPTER WILL COVER THE CONCEPTS AND SCHEMATICS OF SOLAR ELECTRIC SYSTEMS FOR EARTHSHIPS. IT WILL ALSO DISCUSS HOW TO USE A SOLAR ELECTRIC SYSTEM RELATIVE TO THE *PATTERNS AND NATURE OF THE SUN*, AS DISCUSSED IN CHAPTER TWO OF <u>EARTHSHIP VOLUME I</u>. LITTLE ATTENTION WILL BE GIVEN TO SPECIFIC WIRING DETAILS, AS THESE ARE COVERED IN MANY ELECTRICAL WIRING MANUALS ALREADY IN PRINT (see Appendix, Chapter 1). THE OBJECTIVE HERE IS TO PROVIDE THE EARTHSHIP OWNER WITH AN UNDERSTANDING OF THE *NATURE* OF SOLAR ELECTRICITY, HOW IT IS COLLECTED AND STORED, AND HOW TO LIVE WITH IT.

A major design factor of airplanes is to reduce weight so that not as much expensive fuel will be required to fly. A major design factor of solar powered dwellings is to reduce the electrical load demand so that not as much expensive equipment will be required to live. It is not a matter of doing without. It is a matter of **energy-conscious design** *resulting from careful preliminary analysis of both the owner and the dwelling.*

PRELIMINARY ELECTRIC ANALYSIS

Photovoltaic electric systems can be very complicated and almost prohibitively expensive for conventional "energy hog" housing. **Earthships** are a result of energy conscious design and, by their very nature, come a long way toward reducing the electrical requirements of living. Owners, via **energy-conscious living**, can come the rest of the way. The dwelling *and* the owner must be carefully analyzed in terms of electrical requirements placed on the photovoltaic electric system, *before design of the photovoltaic electric system begins.* The purpose being to **reduce the electrical requirements to a minimum via other inherent design features of the dwelling.** The result of this is a minimal solar electric system that will be economically within the grasp of the average homeowner. We can begin this analysis by looking at the systems required for a typical house. We will see why and how they use electricity and then see if we can find a "friend" to provide this energy for free.

HEATING AND/OR COOLING SYSTEMS

Many domestic heating and cooling systems are powered electrically. These systems consume tremendous amounts of electricity. It is not practical to try to get this electricity from the sun with current technology. This would be like trying to pull a train with a huge team of horses - possible maybe, but not practical. Most gas fired domestic heating and cooling systems require electricity of some sort, regardless of the fact that they are fueled by gas. This electricity powers pumps, fans, control panels, etc. These present a *continuous* draw of electricity which would tax a solar powered electrical system. Heating and cooling i.e. (maintaining temperatures near the accepted comfort zone) are **inherent qualities of the Earthship design.** The initial design of the Earthship allows the natural phenomenon of *Thermal Mass* (one of our "friends") to prevail and thereby presents the reality of *avoiding a heating or cooling system of any kind.* Specifically, if you don't break too many of "the rules" outlined in EARTHSHIP Vol. I, you can totally avoid the necessity of a heating or cooling system, and therefore cut out any requirement of electricity for such a system.

4

The initial design of your Earthship plays an important role in determining your electrical needs.

A fireplace, a small, ventless gas heater* or a minimal wood stove (none of which require electricity), strategically placed and used only on rare occasions, is all that an Earthship should ever need for heating. Cooling is handled by venting, shading and proximity to the thermal mass inherently built into the Earthship. The thermal mass of the Earthship is warmer than the winter air and cooler than the summer air. It is a constant equalizer of Earthship temperatures. In all climates, thermal mass (as explained in EARTHSHIP Vol. I, pages 11-13) is "our friend" - a factor of design that can help us completely avoid the use of electricity for heating and cooling. If you want a car that goes fast, you must let aerodynamics prevail in the design. *If you want an Earthship that requires no heating or cooling systems, you must let thermodynamics prevail in the design.* The severity of your heating and/or cooling needs will determine how seriously you must relate to prevailing thermodynamic phenomena in order to avoid any use of electricity for habitat temperature control. Chapter Eight - GRAVITY SKYLIGHTS, has more discussion on ventilation and cooling via natural phenomenon. That chapter further

*1 see Appendix, Chapter 1.

illustrates how **the Earthship itself is its own heating and cooling system.**

WATER SYSTEMS

Conventional water systems, whether community or individual, always require a significant amount of electricity for pumping and pressurization. Consequently, water use can be one of the major load demands upon a domestic photovoltaic electric system. *Design and location of the Earthship, relative to its water system, can reduce and sometimes eliminate this electrical need.* The methods and approaches to Earthship water system design are covered in Chapter Two. They involve four "friends" - Gravity, Sun, Wind and Rain. Again, the point is that, **the initial design of your Earthship, relative to the free and reliable help from natural phenomena, plays an important role in determining your electrical needs.** In Chapter Two we see how one can completely eliminate (or at least drastically reduce) the electrical load demand of water supply and distribution. This can be done with a catchment system integrated into the Earthship design.

DOMESTIC HOT WATER SYSTEMS

Domestic hot water is usually produced by either gas or electricity. The first step here would be to choose gas, as it is more efficient and less devastating to the planet to use than electricity.

However, solar hot water systems can produce a significant amount of domestic hot water, especially in the sun-belt areas. Alternative and more efficient hot water systems are discussed in Chapter Four. The issue at hand is for the home owner to produce hot water via gas power, solar power, or a combination of the two, therefore **avoiding the use of any electricity for hot water production or circulation.** This will require certain design features in your Earthship that must be inherent to the Earthship itself as seen in Chapter Four.

LIGHTING SYSTEMS

The choice and location of lights is a major factor here. Most often, lighting is chosen with aesthetics as the major issue and efficient use of electricity is not even considered. Many light fixtures waste a lot of energy in order to produce "an effect". In a photovoltaic powered Earthship, every light fixture must be examined individually for efficient use of energy and production of light. This will result in dramatic reductions in the energy consumed for lighting. Lighting systems will be discussed in depth in Chapter Five.

The Earthship is inherently flooded with natural light in the daytime via solar windows and skylights. Rarely do any lights need to be used in the daylight hours. This fact, along with careful selection, design and use of night lighting, can result in the Earthship using a fraction of the usual amounts of electricity that a "normal house" uses for lighting.

OTHER SYSTEMS

The following systems do not represent major draws of electricity individually, but they illustrate how much everything we do has become dependent upon electricity and their collective effect is significant. *It is amazing just how much electricity a normal house consumes from various gadgets, pumps, timers, minor systems, and other devices **even when no one is at home.***

Telephones

Since electricity is taken for granted, many phone systems have become dependent upon electricity. A simple telephone does not require household electricity, however, the combination phone/intercom systems, cordless phones, and other auxiliary gadgets related to the phone do require electricity. In most cases this is a small but constant draw of electricity. It is advisable to avoid using these auxiliary telephone gadgets if possible, since they require a constant draw of electricity. The ones that are used should be set up so that one can turn them off and on only when needed, instead of allowing them to constantly use precious electricity. The telephone itself should not be dependent upon electricity.

Intercom systems should be separate from the telephone and have an on/off power switch to conserve power usage.

For totally remote sites with no phone lines, cellular phones similar to the type used in automobiles are required. These require electricity but should be installed with switches for turning power on only when in use. See Appendix this chapter.

Central Vacuum Systems

A central vacuum system is convenient, but it requires a much more powerful motor to create suction over long distances. A small vacuum cleaner that can be carried from room to room uses less electricity for its smaller motor and is preferable. In a large home, a "central vacuum" system should be divided into two or three smaller-motored, sub-central vacuum systems placed in strategic positions throughout the Earthship. These will require less energy for their smaller motors.

Alarm and Security Systems

Many people live where security systems are a must. If this is the case, choose and analyze the system you use, relative to how much and how often it requires electricity. If possible, have it controlled by DC power. When you reduce the amount of equipment dependent on your AC inverter, the smaller and less expensive it will be. Inverters will be defined and discussed on the following pages.

Automatic Watering Systems

Automatic watering systems require control boxes that use electricity. Many electronic control devices have difficulty with AC (110 volt) power converted from DC (12 volt) batteries. Converted AC electricity is not exactly the same as line-grid electricity. The result is that the miniscule circuitry of the control and timing devices do not perform the same way as they would on grid AC power, i.e. devices do not always work how and when they are supposed to. Consequently, DC control boxes are necessary for timed devices such as watering system controls. There are solar powered DC watering systems* on the market that are *independent of the domestic power system*. They have their own solar panels, batteries and DC control boxes. This facilitates keeping the main domestic power system simple, small, inexpensive, and is the recommended way to go. Another important factor of watering systems is the controlled use of "grey water" which allows you to water a planter while brushing your teeth. Grey water systems (discussed in Chapter Three) help reduce the need for automatic watering systems and the resulting electrical demand.

Appliances

All appliances used in solar powered dwellings should be analyzed with regard to constant draws of electricity. For example, many gas ranges require electricity for timers, clocks, burner ignitions, etc. Microwave ovens can come with elaborate timers which draw electricity *all* the time. They also come with simple timers which only use electricity when the unit is being used. The owner of a solar powered home should <u>carefully select which appliances he/she really needs, and then purchase the ones that are OFF when they are not being used.</u> Over 50% of the appliances today still use electricity even when they are not in use.

Do not use electric clocks in a solar home. They are not likely to work well anyway, since the inverted AC power is not "clean" enough for their needs. They are also a constant draw of electricity. There are many other types of clocks available, quartz for example. When there is a choice, *always choose the device which does not need electricity*. This will keep your solar electric system simple and economical.

Conventional electric refrigerators are too inefficient to use in a solar powered home. There are now two DC refrigerators on the market.* They are better insulated, more simple and use

*2 see Appendix, Chapter 1.

much less solar power than conventional models.

Gas refrigerators are also an option, though not as "free" to operate as the DC solar electric models. The <u>Real Goods Catalog</u> (see Appendix Chapter 1) has many energy efficient appliances listed, priced, and reviewed. Solar Survival is currently working on a thermal mass refrigerator that will use even less electricity than the DC refrigerators.

Gas clothes dryers must be used. There is, of course, the timeless and always reliable solar clothes dryer... a clothes line which will work amazingly well year-round inside your Earthship!

Conventional clothes washing machines will work but choose a simple model. The elaborate, deluxe appliances with more gadgets & accessories use more electricity and have more of a problem functioning on the inverted AC power. Dishwashers work also, but, again, a simple model must be chosen. Radios, VCR's, compact disc players and stereos all work on solar power, however, much of this equipment draws power constantly. Your entertainment center should have its own off/on power supply switch which allows you to shut the system off completely when not in use. In many cases a good automobile cassette or compact disc player has been used on a DC circuit just like in your car. This keeps one more appliance from going through your inverter.

OVERALL, THERE ARE SEVERAL THINGS TO REMEMBER WHEN USING APPLIANCES:

1) Think carefully about whether or not an appliance is really needed.
2) Choose non-electric appliances when ever possible.
3) Choose DC appliances when available.
4) Choose an appliance that is really OFF when it says it is "OFF".
5) Do not choose appliances that have many electricity consuming gadgets and accessories - especially timers, brains, etc. which won't work well on inverted power.
6) If an appliance does have a constant draw of power, provide an off/on power supply switch to that appliance.

Our overall objective is to **eliminate, reduce or control** all constant consumption of electricity. The bottom line with the analysis of each of the above systems has been to reduce or eliminate the electrical demands of that system. This involves redesigning the system, re-evaluating owner needs, and in most cases incorporating design features relative to the system into the Earthship itself. **Do not think of the dwelling as separate from its systems.** Think of our bodies. They are a *product* of their various systems - so should the Earthship be a product of its various systems. **The systems are an inherent part of an Earthship.** Regular housing, no matter how elaborate, is usually a box with a variety of energy consuming systems attached to it. The Earthship concept dictates that these systems BE the conceptual building blocks of the dwelling itself. Every system will be discussed in-depth in the following chapters. The purpose here is to establish the fact that analysis of the systems, relative to energy-conscious design and living, and the integration of the systems INTO the Earthship design, results in a **minimal electrical requirement.** This requirement can be economically satisfied by solar power. This is called **DESIGNING DOWN** your energy requirement. Now that we have the solar electrical system itself minimized, we must understand the basics of it and integrate IT into the Earthship design.

THE BASICS OF PHOTOVOLTAIC ELECTRICITY

Energy is gathered via **photovoltaic** panels which convert sunlight into small charges of electricity. This electricity is then delivered to and stored in **batteries.** This is much the same as a tin roof that gathers rain and delivers it to be stored in a barrel.

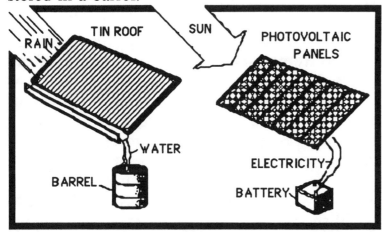

The electricity is gathered and stored as 12 or 24 volt DC current. Most of our appliances are 110 volt AC current, so the electricity that we have captured from the sun must pass through an **inverter**, which changes it from DC to AC power. **The less current that has to go through this inverter, the smaller and less expensive it will be.**

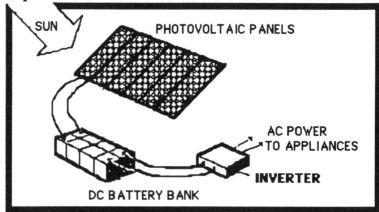

When ALL the power to be used must pass through the inverter, the system becomes *totally dependent* upon the inverter. If the inverter malfunctions, you are without power of any kind. This process of changing DC electricity to AC electricity also results in a loss of about 10% of the energy that has been captured from the sun. Furthermore, the AC inverter can get expensive if it has to handle too much power. These facts have caused many solar energy users to try to use only the DC power. This works well with lighting because there are many DC lights available on the market today. However, currently there are not enough household appliances on the market that work on DC power to satisfy the average person. As a result, sole use of DC power may be too limiting for some people. A combination of the two (DC for lighting and AC for appliances) is a good method of dealing with this situation. With this combination system, if the inverter malfunctions, one still has lights which function directly from the batteries. Also, the lighting system is not subjected to the 10% energy loss caused by converting from DC to AC. The inverter doesn't have to be as large in this set up because lights are not running through it. The DC/AC combination is more efficient, more economical, and somewhat more reliable than a total AC system.

Regular circuit breaker boxes are used in a solar electric system. They occur after the inverter for the AC side of the system and after the batteries in the DC side of the system. From the circuit breaker boxes on, everything else in the system is quite normal. There will be a breaker box for the lights on the DC branch and a breaker box for the appliances on the AC branch, after the inverter.

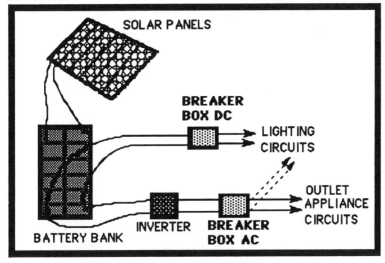

This diagram schematically represents the major factors and flow of a solar electric system. This schematic is over-simplified and is only for understanding the collection, storage and distribution of electricity. Realistically, there are also charge controllers, in-line gauges, main-disconnect switches, and other devices required in a functional schematic. These are available as a **power center** which can include both AC and DC breaker panels.* This unit is designed to provide you with all of the necessary equipment put together in a way that meets electrical codes. In many cases a power center is easier and more economical than installing gauges, breaker panels, disconnects etc. individually.

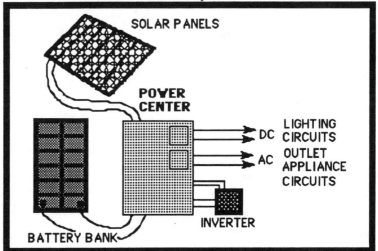

When a power center is used, everything goes into it for total control of the system at one spot.

*3 see Appendix, Chapter 1

One major disconnect for the entire system can be located here. This disconnect shuts off (disconnects) everything.

The gauges in a solar electric system are similar to those on the dashboard of your car. They tell you the condition of your batteries, how much power you are using from your lights and appliances, how much you are getting from the sun, etc. Gauges can be part of the power unit or installed individually. They can be as involved and elaborate as you have money for, or they can be as simple as two or three gauges that, in a flash, can tell you if everything is ok. They should be located in as prominent a place in your Earthship as your fuel gauge is in your car. Gauges are available as remote units and can be placed anywhere in your home, i.e. remote from the room where your power center is.

The DC current is somewhat sluggish compared to the AC current much the same way oil is sluggish when compared to water. Just as the oil requires a much larger pipe to deliver it at a comparable pressure to water, so does DC current require larger wires to deliver at a comparable voltage to AC current. For this reason, in normal applications 10 gauge (heavier) wire is used for DC current, and 12 gauge (lighter) wire is used for AC current. In this situation, the heavier DC circuit for lights can also be used at any time for AC current as AC current works equally well in heavier wire. This allows the entire dwelling to be switched to AC if the owner should so desire and also allows solar dwellings to be wired absolutely conventionally up to the circuit boxes (the heavier wire in the lighting circuits still qualifies as conventional). This is a good idea, since many electricians and code inspectors are not yet familiar with photovoltaics. A conventional house wiring system saves the owner many headaches relative to the inspector's and the electrician's job. The entire photovoltaic system is then considered to be just the POWER SUPPLY to the circuit boxes for a CONVENTIONALLY WIRED DWELLING.

Due to the sluggish DC current, fewer outlets or lights can be put on one circuit in a DC system, than in an AC system. The sluggish DC current will drop in voltage after about three lights or outlets whereas an AC circuit can handle about eight lights or outlets. This is speaking generally, and it ultimately depends upon the actual use the circuit is designed for.

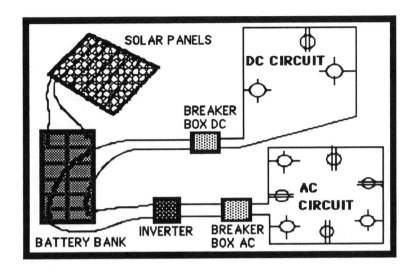

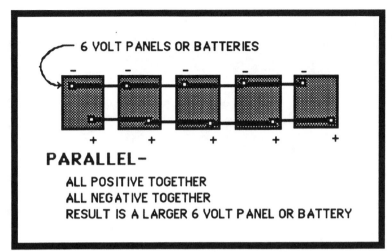

The result is a more powerful six volt battery.

THE COLLECTION PANELS
PHOTOVOLTAIC - VOLTAGE FROM LIGHT

The collection panels come in various sizes, most commonly ranging from 12" x 48" to 18" x 36". The average panel puts out about 40 to 55 watts and costs between $250 to $350. If you shop around, you may find slightly better deals. Sometimes, used panels are available. Since there are no moving parts that wear out in a PV panel, used units are a fairly safe bet. Each panel has a positive and a negative post - just like a battery - and they can be wired in parallel or in series just like batteries. **Parallel** wiring is hooking all the positive posts of a battery or panel together and all of the negative posts together. The following diagram shows many six volt batteries or PV panels wired together with parallel wiring.

Series wiring is a method of changing voltage. For instance - two six volt batteries wired in series results in the sum of the voltages of the two batteries. This is accomplished by wiring the negative post of one to the positive post of the other.

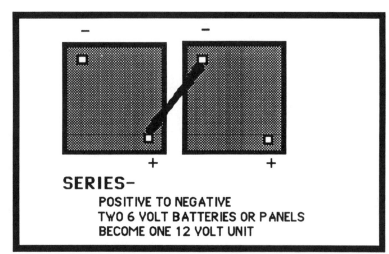

SERIES–

POSITIVE TO NEGATIVE
TWO 6 VOLT BATTERIES OR PANELS
BECOME ONE 12 VOLT UNIT

Heavy gauge wire (#2 or #4 gauge) is needed for both series and parallel wiring of batteries to prevent voltage losses between batteries. <u>Copper end connectors</u> are necessary to connect the heavy wires to the batteries.*

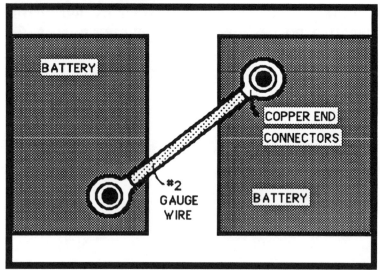

BATTERY

COPPER END
CONNECTORS

#2
GAUGE
WIRE

BATTERY

Most available batteries are 6 volt and most panels

come in 12 volt. Therefore, batteries must be ganged in series to form 12 volts and parallel wired to increase the "size" of the 12 volt batteries.

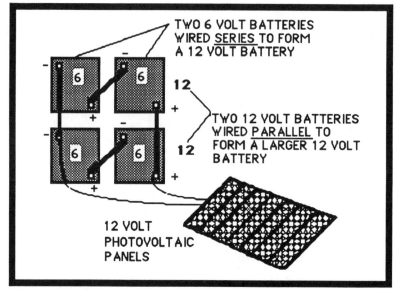

TWO 6 VOLT BATTERIES
WIRED <u>SERIES</u> TO FORM
A 12 VOLT BATTERY

TWO 12 VOLT BATTERIES
WIRED <u>PARALLEL</u> TO
FORM A LARGER 12 VOLT
BATTERY

12 VOLT
PHOTOVOLTAIC
PANELS

Any two six volt batteries can be made into a 12 volt battery via series wiring. The 12 volt batteries can then be wired parallel to become just a larger 12 volt battery.

The panels usually come in 12 volt units. If you "gang" them or wire them in a series, the voltage can be changed from 12 to 24 or 36, etc. This is sometimes necessary, since AC inverters come in 12, 24, and 36 volt units. 12 volt and 24 volt are most common. **The array of panels and the battery bank both have to conform to the**

*4 see Appendix, Chapter 1

voltage of the inverter being used. You could, therefore, have a 12 volt system, 24 volt system, etc. The choice between 12 volts and 24 volts would relate to whether you use all AC power or a combination of AC for outlets and DC for lighting. If you use a combination, a 12 volt system should be used because 12 volt lights are easier to get than 24 volt lights. Further, 24 volt appliances are not as easily available as 12 volt appliances. If you plan to run some lights and a few appliances on DC power, you should go to a 12 volt system, as it is easier to acquire 12 volt appliances and lights. The choice of voltage for your system will also relate to size. Small systems (for a two bedroom home) can easily be 12 volt. Larger homes require larger systems (higher voltage) which get more complicated. For this reason we recommend 2 or 3 small systems (see diagrams page 23) for a larger home. This allows you to stay 12 volt and stay simple. Many engineers and dealers do not yet agree with this. It is easy for an engineer to live with and understand a complex system but the average person would prefer a simple system repeated two or three times in different "wings" of the home.

The panels must face the sun, and so, must have the potential to be adjusted easily (four times a year) in order to be as perpendicular to the sun as possible throughout the seasons of the year - low sun in winter and high sun in the summer (see Earthship Vol. I, Chap. 2). There are many adjustable mounting devices for panels on the market.* It often makes sense to mount the devices directly on the Earthship itself for better proximity to the batteries. Some mounting devices have trackers to follow the sun. This makes it possible to get by with fewer panels, but the cost of the tracker usually offsets any savings for homes in the sun belt. An important issue in mounting is that the panels should not be flat against anything. Panels need air circulation around them to keep cool and sufficient space for wiring behind the panels. The panels must also be kept accessible. There should be no shadows from trees, buildings, chimneys, vents, etc. cast onto the panels at any time of the day, or of the year. One little shadow can "turn off" one whole panel. The panels must be as close as possible to the batteries which are storing the electricity. Due to the sluggishness of the DC electricity collected by the panels, the voltage drop can be significant if there are long distances between panels and batteries. Long distances require very heavy gauge copper wire and *copper is expensive.* For the same reason, batteries should also be centrally located in a large Earthship to avoid long, expensive runs of heavy gauge copper wiring for the dwelling itself. This central

*5 see Appendix, Chapter 1.

location of the batteries will also help to determine the most appropriate and economic location for the panels. The following diagram and photo illustrate a simple Earthship with battery room and adjustable array of photovoltaic panels positioned close to the battery room. This particular Earthship is small, so any location near the building is o.k. In a larger home, the battery room and panels should be more centrally located with respect to all spaces. However, if 2 or 3 small, simple systems are used in a large home, a simple 12 volt system would just be repeated with a nearby battery room for each system.

The PV panels are as integral a part of the Earthship as the headlights on a car. Therefore, they should be treated as such. Many people attempt to hide them. This is possible but always more expensive, inefficient, and inconvenient.

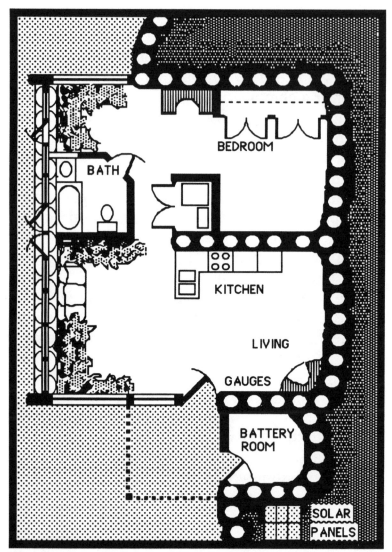

Floor plan of a typical Earthship

THE BATTERIES

The batteries used for storing DC electricity collected from the sun are usually 6 volt deep cycle batteries ganged together with series and parallel wiring in order to create one big 12 or 24 volt battery. This is done in order to relate to whatever kind of AC inverter is being used. Deep cycle means something very similar to a deep barrel of water. Deep cycle batteries hold more charge. There are many types on the market. A six volt battery that lasts about five to seven years will cost about $80. A twelve volt battery that lasts about twenty years will cost about $200. How long a battery lasts depends upon how it is treated. A seven year battery will last seven years ONLY IF IT IS NOT ABUSED. This means that it cannot be overcharged or allowed to be drained too low. Batteries are happiest when they get hot and bubble occasionally. A six volt battery should read as high as 7 to 8 volts (no more) when charging and SHOULD NEVER GET BELOW 6 VOLTS. A twelve volt battery should read from 13 to 15 volts when charging and never dip below 12 volts. If you are constantly draining your batteries they will not last very long. Every system should have an automatic disconnect device to cut the load when the batteries get too low. This same device can cut the solar panel charge of incoming electricity when the batteries are too hot. This device is called a charge controller. For example, in a 12 volt system the charge controller would divert the charge when the voltage reached 15 volts. It would also cut off the load demand from the dwelling when the batteries went down to 11 volts. It is installed between the panels and the batteries or in the power center. Charge controllers are continuing to get smaller, less expensive and more reliable as the industry evolves. They cost about $100 for an average sized house, at this point*. They are an integral part of the power center described on page 11. They can also be purchased and installed individually.

All batteries must have their water checked about once every month. This is similar to checking the water in your car battery. There are electronic devices that will alert you when your batteries are low on water. If you do not have this device, then checking the battery water is your trade off for not having an electric bill. Batteries should be filled only with distilled water.

Batteries must be kept in a <u>room temperature</u> environment in order to function at optimum efficiency. **A battery room becomes an important, centrally located factor in any "off the grid" Earthship design.** This room must be kept well-vented and separate from any other electrical or plumbing equipment such as

*6 see Appendix, Chapter 1

the inverter or the hot water heaters. The batteries actually <u>need a space of their own</u>. It can be a separated, vented section (or box) in a mechanical room but there should be enough space to easily check and top off battery the water.

THE INVERTER

There are many inverters on the market. Size is a big issue with any inverter. If the power requirement is *DESIGNED DOWN* through the analysis discussed earlier, the inverter can be kept smaller and, obviously, less expensive. Some inverters can be "ganged" like batteries and solar panels. This is an important factor to consider when purchasing an inverter as it allows your system to grow. Expect to spend $1,100 for an inverter large enough to handle a small home with a *DESIGNED DOWN* power load. The inverter must be kept very close to the batteries due to the voltage drop in the "sluggish" DC current. However, it must be in a separate space from the batteries as a spark from the inverter could cause an explosion in the batteries. Usually battery rooms have a special compartment for batteries and all the other breaker panels, inverter, etc are in the battery room but OUTSIDE the vented battery compartment.

The panels, the batteries, the inverter and the gauges (or the power center including circuit panel gauges and controller) are the main components of a photovoltaic power system. This is very simple for an average two or three bedroom electrically *DESIGNED DOWN* home. Larger homes get more complicated but still use these basic components. S.S.A. or Photocomm Inc. (see Appendix Chapter 1) should be consulted for systems larger than eight panels and ten batteries. S.S.A. currently recommends a series of small eight panel, 10 battery systems for a larger home. We recommend this because we know the cost and performance of the small system. It is therefore very easy to project cost and performance for 2, 3 or 4 of these. Larger systems can get out of control on unforeseen costs, design fees, electricians' dilemmas, maintenance and service, and questionable performance.

BACKUP

Learning to sail a boat takes practice. Likewise, living in a solar home takes practice. An experienced solar fanatic could take a small photovoltaic system and never have a problem or a care. However, an inexperienced believer who has spent all of his or her life with an abundance of power could get into trouble quite often during the first year or so of solar living. Good advice to the novice is to have a backup source of power if possible. This is to avoid inconvenience and to save and prolong the life of the batteries in case of an unusual number of cloudy days. There is also the possibility of leaving something on and running down your system. Wind becomes second nature to the sailor but all of us are not sailors yet. A backup system can make learning to "sail with the sun" a more pleasant experience.

Gasoline or propane generators are one method of backing up a system. Another method is simply having an electric hookup that you switch on only for emergency use. <u>Both methods of backup should be set up to charge the batteries only</u>, just as the sun charges the batteries. This way you will always be using the same system. There are "brains" that cost about $700 to control this automatically.* If you are using a series of small systems, just have the backup go to one strategic system to provide backup in one main area.

Photovoltaic systems for a two bedroom home can be as small as eight panels, ten batteries, an eleven-hundred dollar inverter and a few simple gauges , i.e. $5000 or $6000 with a power center. The same home if not properly analyzed or *"Designed Down"*, with an owner *unable to evolve* from *"gadget dependence""* could need a $20,000 system. The issues here are **analysis**, **energy-conscious design** and **personal evolution.** These three ingredients can work

*7 and 8 see Appendix, Chapter 1

together to make independence the way sand, cement and water work together to make concrete.

Larger homes need not be more complicated. They can be broken up into "wings", each with its own simple eight panel power system or in some cases ganging two together. This keeps the systems simple and easy to understand. Coordinating and integrating the systems of the various wings may still need guidance by S.S.A.*

LIVING WITH A SOLAR ELECTRIC SYSTEM

The bulk of this chapter has provided a basic understanding of photovoltaic electrical systems. This understanding must be established in order to attempt living with a PV system. Now that we understand what we are trying to live with, *let's live with it*.

You get up in the morning. It's cloudy. O.K., you're not going to do a wash today. You don't turn up the heat because your Earthship inherently provides it. You don't need any lights during the daylight hours for the same reason. As a matter of fact, you don't need *any* power today except for a few small things. You're going to get a few FAX messages, so you turn on your FAX machine as needed. Your solar refrigerator is running, but it is so well insulated and efficiently designed that it can run off and on for several days without really depleting your power system. If there are many cloudy days, a solar refrigerator can be turned off at night and then back on in the morning without spoiling the food. This is possible only because it is so well insulated. The new "mass solar" refrigerators by Solar Survival will allow this as a normal procedure. You need your computer, but it doesn't use that much power and your battery bank is sized to handle this small load for several days. You watch the weather report to see if it's going to be cloudy or sunny for the next few days. (The weather man is getting more and more reliable as the years pass by). If it's going to be cloudy, you don't use many lights tonight and you keep T.V. viewing to a minimum. If it's going to be sunny tomorrow, you plan to do a wash tomorrow, and maybe you'll watch a video movie.

The point is that you stay in tune with the weather and you plan your daily activities accordingly. This is not too much of a problem given the fact that all of your power and household energy is absolutely free for the rest of your life. Your only obligation is that you stay in tune with the daily weather forecast to plan your day, as opposed to doing whatever you want, whenever you want, as often as you want, and having to pay for it through the nose with both money and

destruction of the environment. *Who cares if your kids still have a planet to live on as long as you can do a wash whenever you want and can run the dishwasher so you don't risk getting dish-pan hands?* The idea here is to know that **you will still live through your children after your body is dead and gone.** It's like you have a sandwich and your two kids are with you. Would you eat it all and tell them to find their own, or would you divide it into three pieces and give them each some of it? Well, it's the same with this earth. Do we want to leave some for our children or do we want to *eat the whole thing ourselves?*

When the sun is out, you use as much electricity as you want. When it is cloudy you watch what you do - **or else you fight wars over oil and live with nuclear waste.** That is all there is to it. You watch the weather and your gauges and decide what you want to do and when you want to do it. The sun is your friend, a dependable friend. You know its nature - it is sometimes behind a cloud. You can depend on this also. It's almost like a relationship with another person. This person has moods. The sun has "moods" but unlike another person, it has no ego. We accept the seasons ("moods") for what they are. We ski in the winter and sunbathe in the summer. This is the same attitude we must adopt on a *daily basis* for solar living. Our lives must *gravitate* around the sun, much the same as the planets *gravitate* around the sun. We allow our lives to gravitate around much shallower things like TV shows, religions, social clubs, football games, politics etc. Why not let something as true, unbiased, reliable and giving as the sun call a few of the shots? This is all it takes to live free of utility bills and with the promise of having a planet for our children to inherit.

Solar living is much the same as sailing in a sailboat. The boat is designed to relate to the wind. The boat is operated relative to what the wind is doing. The good sailor still goes wherever he wants without noise, without pollution, without fear, but with the peace of mind in knowing there will always be wind.

Solar Survival Recommendations

Our recommendations are based on twenty years of trial and error in solar living. The technology is constantly evolving and we are constantly learning. These recommendations may be subject to change every six months as we continue to put ourselves in "guinea pig" situations to learn more through further testing of current equipment, as well as testing our concepts (of how to use that equipment) and ourselves.

For an average 2 to 3 bedroom *DESIGNED DOWN* home:

Panels
> 8 Kyocera 51 watt panels with pole mount rack

Batteries
> 10 to 12 Exide or Trojan 6 volt deep cycle batteries. We do not currently recommend twenty year expensive batteries as technology will be radically improved in seven years. Why be stuck with a 20 year battery?

Inverter
> Photocomm PCUL 12/17 2500 watt inverter. UL continuous output 1700 watts

Charge controller
> Photocomm NDR 30 12 volt with manual override usually built in to power center.

Power center
> Custom order from S.S.A. This unit will include the main disconnect required by code as well as amp and voltage meters, AC and DC circuit breaker boxes, charge control and panel disconnects.

The power center described above is a code approved unit that allows you (via diagrams) to hook up your own inverter, batteries and panels to this unit. All the technical electronics work that would require an electrician is done for you inside this unit. You simply custom order the power center with the number of AC and/or DC circuits you want.

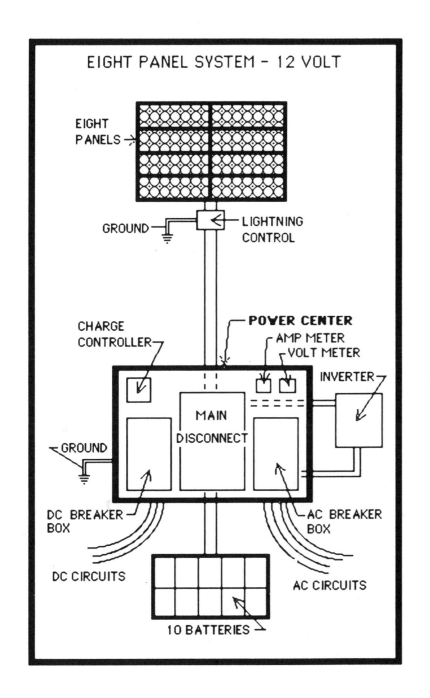

EIGHT PANEL SYSTEM - 12 VOLT

EIGHT PANELS →

GROUND — LIGHTNING CONTROL

CHARGE CONTROLLER

POWER CENTER

AMP METER
VOLT METER

INVERTER

GROUND

MAIN DISCONNECT

DC BREAKER BOX

AC BREAKER BOX

GROUND

DC CIRCUITS

AC CIRCUITS

10 BATTERIES

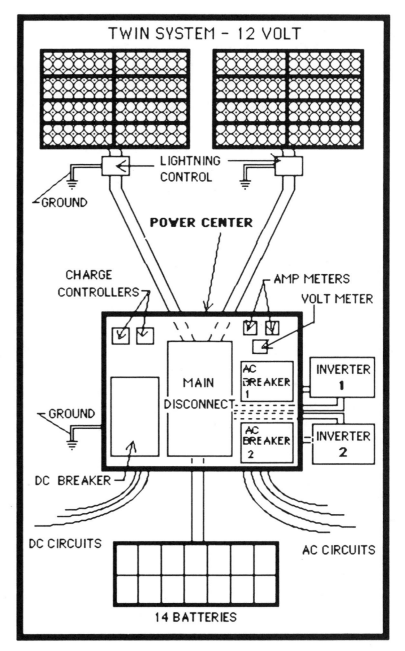

TWIN SYSTEM - 12 VOLT

LIGHTNING CONTROL

GROUND

POWER CENTER

CHARGE CONTROLLERS

AMP METERS
VOLT METER

MAIN DISCONNECT

AC BREAKER 1

INVERTER 1

GROUND

AC BREAKER 2

INVERTER 2

DC BREAKER

DC CIRCUITS

AC CIRCUITS

14 BATTERIES

Larger Homes

Break the home up into "wings and use several modules of either or both of the systems diagrammed on the previous page integrated by SSA. Larger "designed" systems can get out of hand on cost and complications very easily. Furthermore, they are hard to understand and service for average home owners and electricians. This small system has proven itself as a reliable, simple and strong system and we know exactly what it costs. Simply duplicating it for a large dwelling (with some technical advice from SSA) is a safe and simple recommendation. Many solar engineers might not agree with this but our recommendation comes from living with and using solar energy for many years - we are currently building a community with modules of this system as the power supply for construction tools - jack hammers, concrete mixers, skillsaws, sanders, etc. When construction is complete, the same system that built the home powers it.

APPENDIX

Ventless Gas Heaters
MADE BY VALOR
Order from Solar Survival Architecture
505 758-9870
PO Box 1041 Taos, New Mexico 87571

1. Small - will serve as a backup heater for up to 600 square feet of Earthship space.
184-N for natural gas
184-P for LP gas

2. Large - will serve as a backup heater for up to 1000 square feet of Earthship space.
185-N for natural gas
185-P for LP gas

Solar Watering Systems

1. Photocomm, Inc.
   Landscape/Irrigation Division
   1941 Don Lee Place, Suite B
   Escondido, CA 92025
   (619) 741-5690

or

   Photocomm, Inc.
   Solar Electric Power Systems
   4419 E. Broadway
   Tucson, AZ 85711
   (602) 327-8558

2. Rain Bird Sales, Inc.
   145 North Grand Avenue
   Glendora, CA 91740
   (818) 963-9311

3. Sprinkler Irrigation Supply Company
   4610 McLead Road, N.E.
   Albuquerque, NM 87109 (505) 881-4050

Solar refrigerators
MADE BY SUN FROST
Available from 4 cubic foot to 19 cubic foot
Order from Solar Survival Architecture (SSA)
  Box 1041
  Taos, NM 87571
  (505) 758-9870

Photovoltaic Panels, Mounting Racks, Charge Controllers, Inverters, Control Brains, Power Centers and Batteries.
Order from Solar Survival Architecture (SSA)
  Box 1041
  Taos, NM 87571
  (505) 758-9870

Wiring Manuals for Solar Electric Systems
1. New Solar Electric Home
   by Joel Davidson

2. Living on 12 Volts and Wiring 12 Volts
   for Ample Power
   by David Smead and Ruth Ishihara

3. Wiring Simplified
   by H.P. Richter

4. Home Power Magazine
   P.O. Box 130
   Hornbrook, CA 96044 - 0130

Solar pumps
MADE BY SURE FLOW
Order from Solar Survival Architecture (SSA)
  Box 1041
  Taos, NM 87571
  (505) 758-9870

2. Photocomm, Inc.
   Solar Electric Power Systems
   4419 E. Broadway
   Tucson, AZ 85711
   (602) 327-8558

3. Flowlight Solar Power Workshop
   Rte. 1 Box 216
   Espanola, NM 87532
   1-800-DC-SOLAR

Cellular Phones
  Decker Communications Systems
  P.O. Box 2298
  201 Cruz Alta Rd.
  Taos, NM 87571

Consultation for all Systems
  By appointment, phone or in person @ $60/hr
  Solar Survival Architecture (SSA)
  Box 1041
  Taos, NM 87571
  (505) 758-9870

26

2. DOMESTIC WATER
S Y S T E M S

IN THESE TIMES IT IS BEST TO HAVE AND TO BE IN CONTROL OF YOUR OWN WATER SUPPLY. MOST CITY, TOWN AND COMMUNITY WATER SYSTEMS (IN ADDITION TO PROVIDING "QUESTIONABLE" WATER) ARE DEPENDENT ON ELECTRICITY FOR OBTAINING AND DELIVERING WATER. THIS MAKES THE **WATER DEPENDENT ON COMMERCIAL ELECTRICITY.** COMMERCIAL ELECTRICITY LOOKS UNRELIABLE FOR THE FUTURE EVEN IF YOU CAN OVERLOOK THE DEVASTATION THAT PRODUCING CENTRALIZED COMMERCIAL ELECTRICITY BRINGS. *THEREFORE AN EARTHSHIP MUST HAVE ITS OWN WATER SYSTEM.*

THIS CHAPTER WILL COVER WAYS OF ACQUIRING AND DELIVERING WATER THAT USE MINIMAL OR NO ELECTRICITY. AS IN THE PREVIOUS CHAPTER THE FOCUS WILL BE ON THE METHODOLOGY AND CONCEPT IN AN ATTEMPT TO ESTABLISH A CLEAR UNDERSTANDING OF *HOW TO GET GOOD WATER* FOR DOMESTIC USE. THE EQUIPMENT NEEDED WILL BE DISCUSSED BUT ACTUAL INSTALLATION OF THE EQUIPMENT, WHICH INVOLVES CONVENTIONAL PLUMBING AND MECHANICAL SKILLS, WILL BE ASSUMED TO BE WITHIN THE GRASP OF LOCAL MECHANICAL CONTRACTORS AND OTHER CONSULTANTS.

*Water was a major factor in bringing life to the earth. Water rises, falls, runs and travels all over the earth in many different forms - vapor, rivers, rain etc. Water joins and embraces the earth and the result is a beauty and a life force that far surpasses what the earth would be without water. Maybe humans should learn something from water. Does our interaction with the earth result in something that far surpasses what the earth would be like without us or **would the earth be better off without us?***

Water is much like electricity and money. If you need a tremendous amount of it, it becomes difficult to acquire and you find yourself devastating something or someone else to get it However if your requirements are minimal your quest for water will be an easy one with little effect on the other inhabitants of the planet.

With this thought in mind let's look at the water requirements for a typical house.

PRELIMINARY WATER ANALYSIS

A conventional house is set up as if water supplies were endless. Many areas (California) are beginning to see that this is not true. Water tables that took thousands of years to develop are being lowered not to return in the foreseeable future. Water tables and bodies of surface water are being contaminated by everything from sewage, pesticides and garbage dumps to power plants and industry. Much of the water in the future will have to be purified which will be a time consuming and expensive process, if adequate water is available at all. Due to potential water shortage and existing contamination of water, individual dwellings must capture, purify and reuse their own water. **The Earthship must have features inherent to the initial design to achieve this.** Looking at the various water uses in an existing house is the place to start assimilating information for designing a water system into the Earthship.

TOILETS

Toilets take 4 to 5 gallons of water every time they are flushed. Not only is this an excessive waste of water, it also presents a problem of what to do with this 5 gallons of water that is now raw sewage. If we didn't mix our shit with so much water it would be a whole lot easier to deal with as it would be a much smaller quantity of matter. Toilet or "black water" systems will be dealt with in the next chapter. The issue here is to point out that the use of large quantities of water for dealing with our shit is ridiculous and ultimately makes the problem worse, aside from using too much water. We simply do not have the water to waste anymore considering the contamination, the shortage and the energy and effort it takes to obtain water and, in the future, purify it.

Consequently, it is advisable to use composting type toilets which (believe it or not) *are* developed to the point that they work well and do not smell. They also give you something to put back into the soil. **The use of compost toilets immediately makes a significant reduction in your water requirement.**

There are various types of compost toilets, some of which even flush requiring a small amount (1 quart) of water. There are also low flush type toilets which use a fraction (1 gal.) of the water that a conventional toilet uses. These are all steps in the right direction. However the best advice considering all factors is to **not use water for a toilet at all** (sources for composting toilets are presented in the appendix for this chapter).

SHOWERS AND BATHS

There is no doubt that the grime and dirty air of city living gets both clothes and people dirtier much faster than the cleaner air and cleaner life, in general, of rural living. *Less pollution would therefore enable us to use less water to stay clean.* As we continue to create a dirtier world, we continue to increase our demand for water. This, coupled with our water-related luxuries has resulted in a tremendous water per capita figure for the average American. A normal modern household is equipped to facilitate long steamy showers and/or deep sudsy baths for every individual once or twice a day. This is not to mention the more luxurious homes with hot tubs, jacuzzis and swimming pools. There is a question here. Is there enough water on the planet (and sewage facilities) for every one on the planet to be this luxurious with water? This is not a moral issue. It is a *fact* of humanity. Whether we like it or not humanity is a *unit*. Just as water seeks a common level and will not rest until it does - so does humanity seek a common level and will not rest until it does. **There will not be peace on earth until all of humanity has reached a common level.** No more "haves" and "have-nots", upper class and lower class, privileged and not privileged. We must therefore use this earth and everything on it with all the rest of our "human unit" in mind. If everyone can not do what you are doing then the the very fact that you are doing it is not in keeping with ecology, peace, or common sense.

Even if you do not see yourself connected to all of humanity, the excessive use of water simply makes it harder for you to obtain and deliver your own water and thus makes you and your lifestyle more dependent on a very shaky if not outright disintegrating way of life. The bottom line here is fewer and shorter showers with water saving shower heads, fewer baths in smaller bathtubs, and *communal* swimming and jacuzzi facilities. The idea of communal anything is totally distasteful to some people, but just how many of your amenities do you think you can individually own? After all, we are *communally* sharing this planet. The Romans had "The Baths" and they were quite beautiful. Do we all need our own swimming pools, jacuzzis, and hot tubs? **The use of water, like the use of electricity, has gotten out of hand when "American standards" are translated to a global level. <u>Reduce *your* requirement and reduce *everyone's* stress.</u>**

One doesn't have to agree with the thoughts put forth above to at least understand that the amount of water used for bathing could be cut in half thereby making it much easier to obtain and deliver your own water.

SINKS

The way we use sinks is their only problem. Most all of the operations that we do at kitchen and bathroom sinks waste water. Water is left running while we shave or while we wash dishes. It simply goes down the drain increasing our sewage problem and decreasing our water supply. Getting into the frame of mind that **water is like energy, gold/money, or time** will help us use our sinks in such a way that we will significantly reduce our water consumption.

PLANTS, GARDENS AND LANDSCAPING

Most interior planting and gardening can and should be watered with re-used grey water. This will be discussed in the following chapter. Landscaping and tree planting should seriously relate to indigenous life that thrives on existing climatic conditions, i.e. rainfall. Mulch should be used both inside and out to conserve and hold the water used for plants. Obviously it takes a certain amount of water to start and transplant things, but once they are established **landscaping should not require constant watering**. For example, if you build an Earthship in the desert and try to grow a huge lawn you are creating stress for yourself and the planet. Lawns are *out* if you are trying to provide your own water in a climate where grass doesn't grow naturally. **Water-conscious landscaping must prevail** (and can be very original and beautiful) if you want to survive on your own water system. It may not even be a question of whether you want to or not anyway - you may *have* to survive on your own water system. *Then its you or the grass.*

OTHER USES OF WATER

Everything else from washing the car to washing the dog to hosing the driveway will want to be thought about before you do it. There are many ways we use water and take it for granted. If we were supplying our own water (at no expense to ourselves or the planet) most of these ways we use water would probably be dropped from our schedule without remorse.

It is quite clear that less pollution, trimming and/or organizing our luxuries, and simply assuming a *water -conscious way of life* could cut our consumption of water by 75%. If we can make this mental shift*, we can reduce our water requirement to the point that it will be within our grasp to acquire and deliver it to ourselves.

Now that we have reduced/designed down our water requirement to something within our grasp, let's look at how to go about getting it.

THE BASICS OF ACQUIRING AND DISTRIBUTING WATER

CONVENTIONAL WELLS
Conventional wells are pumped with a submersible electric pump to a pressure tank which pressurizes the water lines for household use.

*1 see <u>A Coming of Wizards</u>, p.106.

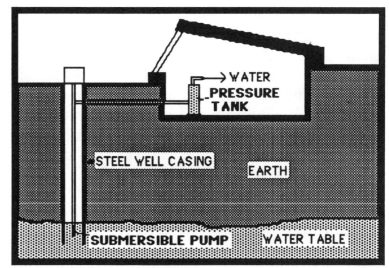

This requires electricity to pump from the well and pressurize the tank every time a significant amount of water is used. Well pumps use a lot of electricity because they are pumping from deep in the well. They use even more when they first start up. This is called a surge. Therefore, **serious electricity is needed every time water is needed.** When you are making your own electricity, it is precious. *You can reduce and in some cases avoid the use of electricity every time you use water.*

SOLAR WELL AND CISTERN
A conventional well can be pumped into a storage cistern continuously and slowly all day long (while the sun is out) by a small solar powered DC pump. The surge is avoided because the pump is not turned of and on all day. It only

comes on once and goes off once a day. Storage of electricity in batteries is avoided because the small pump only has to run while the sun is out. The pump can be very small because it doesn't have to produce waterline pressure from deep in the well. It simply has to trickle water into the cistern all day long. The water is then pumped from the cistern into a conventional pressure tank which pressurizes the water lines for domestic use. This pump is DC and also is much smaller and uses much less electricity than the conventional AC pump deep in the well. Therefore, this method reduces the amount of electricity used every time water is needed as the <u>two small pumps</u> use much less electricity than the <u>one large pump</u> (see Appendix, Chapter 2 for solar pumps). DC pumps are advisable as they do not require an inverter. (see Chapter One)

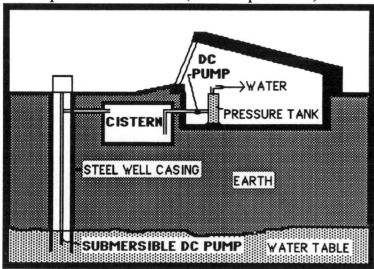

With this system you are getting water pumped for free whenever the sun is out without depleting your battery storage of electricity for domestic use. You can then use this water anytime of the day or night with a *small* amount of your solar electricity from your battery bank. This has become a standard method of obtaining water for "off the grid" dwellings. This is a better way but it still requires electricity (even though a much smaller amount) every time you use water.

SOLAR WELL - GRAVITY CISTERN
With a little help from one of our friends - **gravity** - we can eliminate one of the electric pumps and the pressure tank. If you have chosen a sloped building sight (and this is a good reason to do so) you can solar pump the water from the well into a storage cistern placed up the hill from the Earthship and let gravity provide pressure and delivery of the water to the dwelling.

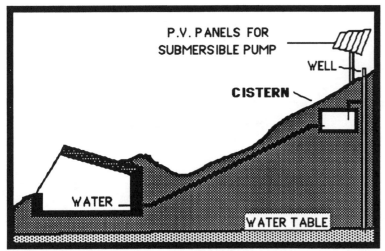

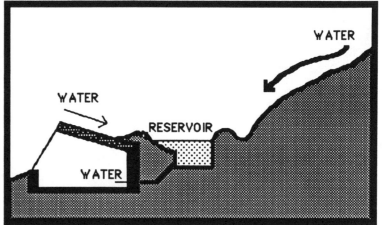

This concept can also be applied exactly the same way using a common windmill instead of solar panels and a pump. Just as our friend the sun "lives" in the sky, **gravity "lives" on a sloped site.** Choosing a sloped site is choosing a site with *built in energy* for domestic water distribution and waste water distribution as we will see in the following chapter. This built in energy can also aid in the collection of water which can eliminate the well and/or pumping process altogether.

WATER CATCHES

With a little forethought in site selection and Earthship-landscape design, you can avoid the well *and* the pump by catching roof run-off and/or hillside run-off in a reservoir or cistern. Locate your reservoir or cistern as high as possible and your plumbing as low as possible and

The price (after initial installation) is free forever. Gravity is a phenomenon like the sun. It continuously gives. We simply have to "position ourselves" appropriately to receive. This is the nature of this vessel we call Earthship. It will sail without stress forever. We will never run out of sun or gravity and we will never have to pay for them in any fashion.

In this case rain and gravity completely eliminate the need for electricity in the water system. Again we see that **the initial design of your Earthship is interwoven with the various systems themselves.**

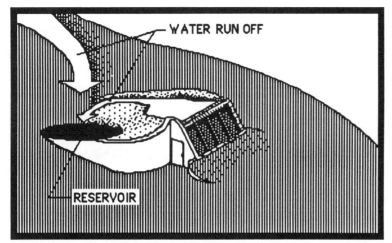

With conservative use of water the above system can fully provide for the water needs of a dwelling even in areas with only occasional rainfall. If you are catching surface run-off from the entire mountain or hill behind you, a tremendous amount of water can be caught from each rainfall.

Reservoirs that catch ground surface run-off need silt catches to trap dirt and gravel from the water. One way to do this is to build a small dam in front of the cistern with a small pool behind it. This blocks the runoff and lets the water overflow into the cistern after particles etc. have settled to the bottom of the silt catch. This simply lets settlement to take place before the water reaches the cistern.

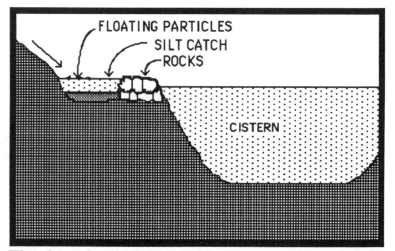

The dam should have rocks on top at the point of overflow. The water can flow through the rock to filter out particles floating on top.

Another method filters the water through rock barriers ranging from large boulders to gravel on the way to the cistern.

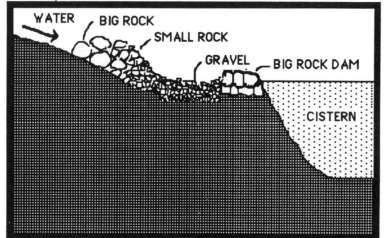

Even with silt catchers, outdoor cisterns still get some debris on top and silt on the bottom. This, in addition to a potential layer of ice on the surface, requires a "floating intake" from the cistern to keep the intake pipe away from debris on top and silt on the bottom.

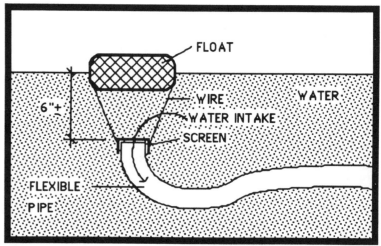

Here the flexible intake pipe is suspended to the desired distance below the surface and above the bottom.

Water catch cisterns should be placed on south facing slopes in cold climates to catch snow melt. On north slopes the ice and snow evaporate before melting thus losing most of the water to the sky.

Insulated floating spa covers would be required to cover your water reservoir during the freezing winter months. Another option is to build a structure/room over the reservoir and use it for a humid growing space while protecting your water from freezing.

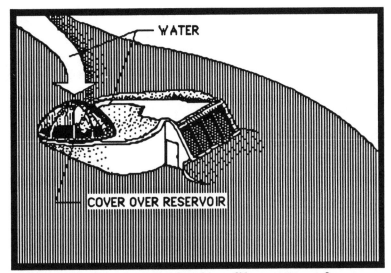

WATER

COVER OVER RESERVOIR

In line filters are required to filter water from an open cistern. These filters require some pressure to suck the water through. A small DC solar booster pump can be used here (see Appendix, Chapter 2 for DC pumps and filters).

ROOF CATCHES

In areas with reasonable rainfall, enough water for domestic use can be caught from the roof alone. If you have at least 10" of precipitation per year, your roof is all the collection you would need. (see appendix for annual rainfall-National Weather Service) Collecting roof runoff is much easier and more economical than collecting ground surface runoff. It requires a metal roof for drinking water. The rubber (Brai) roofs presented in <u>Earthship, Volume I</u> can be painted with one coat of epoxy or acrylic paint and then

one coat of Livos paint* to make the collected water potable. The following diagram illustrates a water catch system that will work in most of the U.S.A.

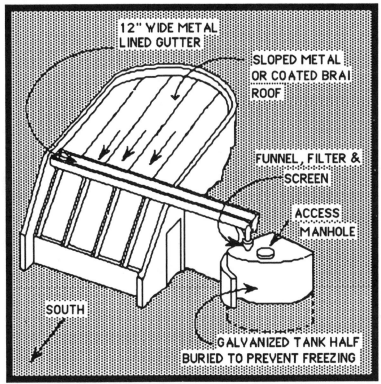

12" WIDE METAL LINED GUTTER

SLOPED METAL OR COATED BRAI ROOF

FUNNEL, FILTER & SCREEN

ACCESS MANHOLE

SOUTH

GALVANIZED TANK HALF BURIED TO PREVENT FREEZING

The water is caught by the south pitched (metal or coated) roof. It is then collected in the south facing gutter and runs to the storage tank. The storage tank* is partially submerged to create enough thermal mass to prevent hard freezing of the water.

*2 An organic paint, see Appendix, Chapter 2
*3 see Appendix, Chapter 2

The water is then pumped into the dwelling by way of an underground line (below frost level) with a small D.C., solar powered pump. The solar pump pressurizes a conventional pressure tank, and the result is typical household water from the tap. Use <u>conservatively</u>. An in-line filter is required before the pump to protect it.

Two people use about 800 gallons of water per month when compost toilets and grey water systems are employed. Therefore a 3,000 gallon reservoir would take you through almost four months without precipitation (see Appendix, Chapter 2 for galvanized tanks). A galvanized tank should be painted with tar on the outside part that is buried. This helps prevent rust and corrosion. The partial burial of the tank captures enough thermal mass to prevent freezing of the water. If you get less than 10" of precipitation per year in your area, install two or three 3000 gallon tanks to catch more from each rain. A tank larger than 3000 gallons gets difficult to handle.

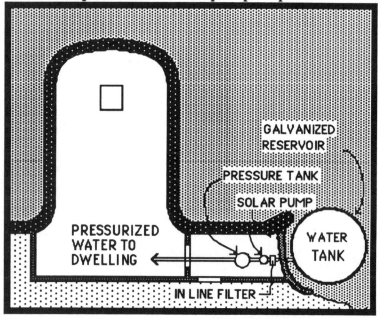

CATCHING WATER FROM SNOW

The standard design of the Earthship, presented in Volume 1, must be slightly modified in order to catch snow melt. **The roof must slope to the south.** This causes the snow to melt faster than it evaporates. A roof that slopes north will lose two-thirds of your snow to evaporation before it melts.

*4 see Appendix, Chapter 2.

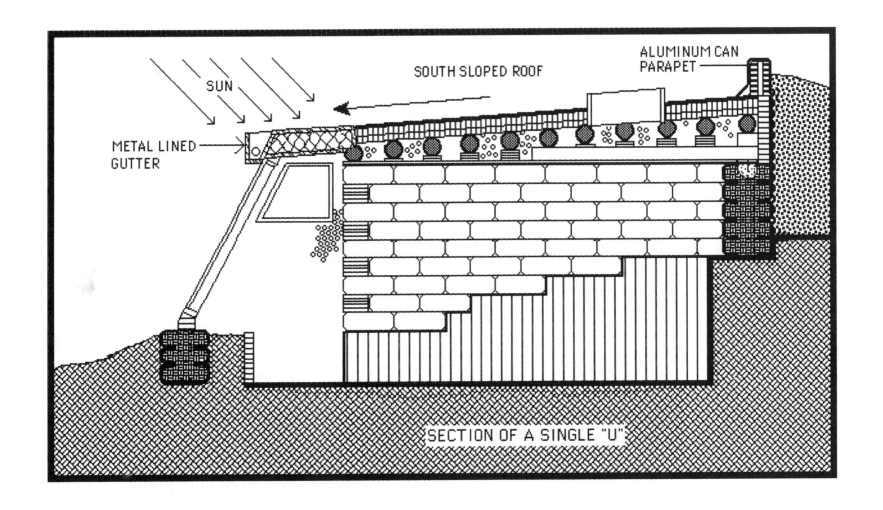

SUN

METAL LINED
GUTTER

SOUTH SLOPED ROOF

ALUMINUM CAN
PARAPET

SECTION OF A SINGLE "U"

The slight north pitch of the roof presented in Volume 1 will allow snow to evaporate before it melts, thus losing most of your water to the sky. The south pitch described here, facilitates melting and reduces the possibility of ice dams.

This south pitch is structured similar to the north pitch, as the above diagram illustrates. The aluminum can parapet is recommended to keep bermed-up dirt off the roof.

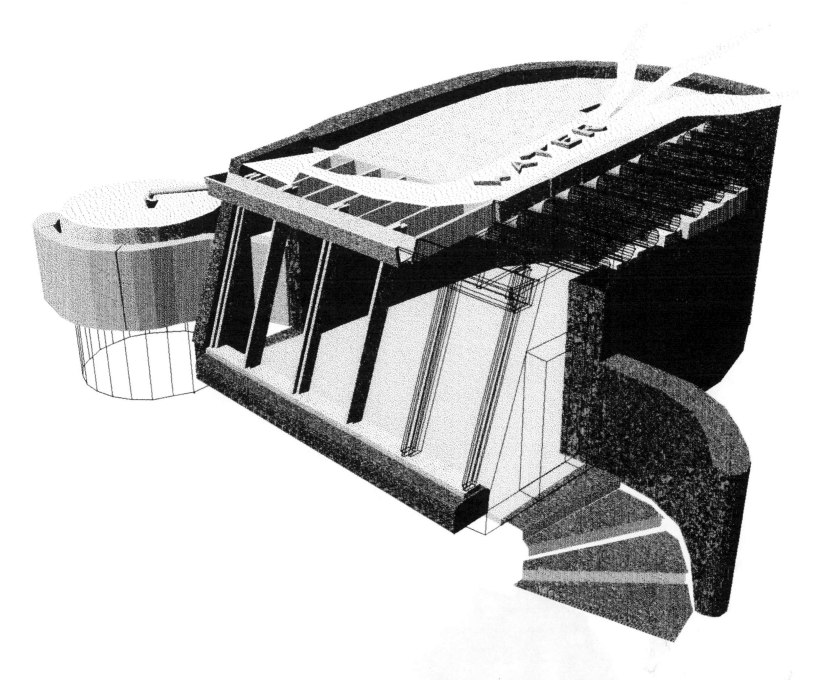

40

Screens should be used where the gutter drains into the pipe that goes to the storage tank to begin filtering out debris.

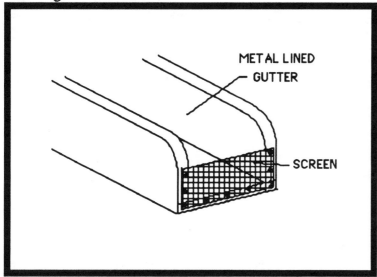

METAL LINED
GUTTER

SCREEN

As the pipe drains into the tank, a metal funnel (as large as possible)with a vegetable screen basket (or some homemade facsimile) can further collect any debris.

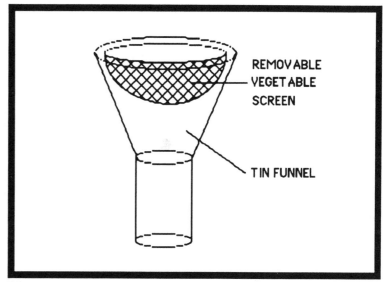

REMOVABLE
VEGETABLE
SCREEN

TIN FUNNEL

The size of this funnel and screen is relative to the roof collection surface. A larger roof area requires a larger funnel and tank inlet. In some cases this will get so large that the vegetable screen basket will have to be fabricated to a large custom size. The larger you make your funnel and inlet pipe the less chance there is of having a torrential rain overflow your funnel and waste some water. We recommend at least a 3" inlet into the tank.

Any fiber or filtering material such as common pillow stuffing can be used to further filter the water as it falls into the tank. The diagram on the next page shows a good preliminary filtering set-up.

41

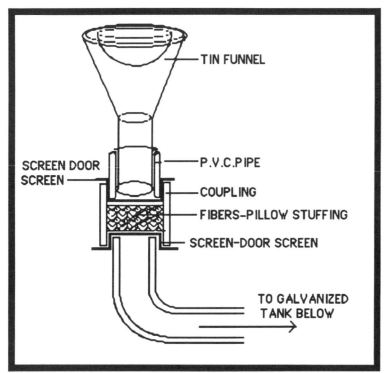

TIN FUNNEL

SCREEN DOOR SCREEN

P.V.C.PIPE

COUPLING

FIBERS-PILLOW STUFFING

SCREEN-DOOR SCREEN

TO GALVANIZED TANK BELOW

A regular in-line filter* should be installed between the storage tank and any pumps. Most pumps have specifications for protective filters required. Catching run-off from the mountain or hill itself <u>in addition</u> to the roof requires more filters after the pump. A special drinking water filter that filters out bacteria may be necessary. Have your water tested to determine this. The following two diagrams illustrate the plumbing schematic for a "clean catch" requiring less filters and a "dirty catch" requiring more filters.

*5 See Appendix, Chapter 2

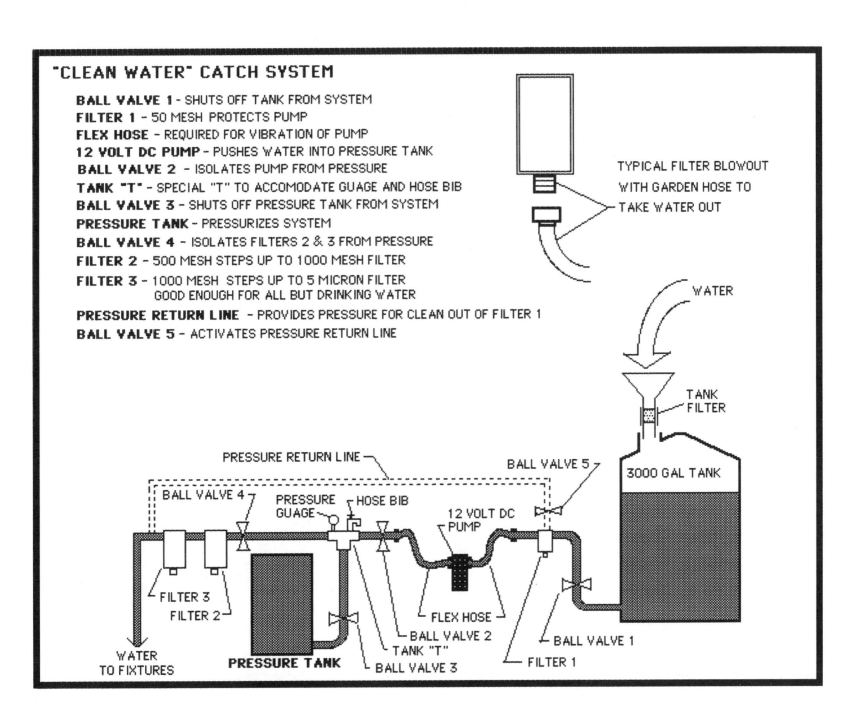

"CLEAN WATER" CATCH SYSTEM

BALL VALVE 1 - SHUTS OFF TANK FROM SYSTEM

FILTER 1 - 50 MESH PROTECTS PUMP

FLEX HOSE - REQUIRED FOR VIBRATION OF PUMP

12 VOLT DC PUMP - PUSHES WATER INTO PRESSURE TANK

BALL VALVE 2 - ISOLATES PUMP FROM PRESSURE

TANK "T" - SPECIAL "T" TO ACCOMODATE GUAGE AND HOSE BIB

BALL VALVE 3 - SHUTS OFF PRESSURE TANK FROM SYSTEM

PRESSURE TANK - PRESSURIZES SYSTEM

BALL VALVE 4 - ISOLATES FILTERS 2 & 3 FROM PRESSURE

FILTER 2 - 500 MESH STEPS UP TO 1000 MESH FILTER

FILTER 3 - 1000 MESH STEPS UP TO 5 MICRON FILTER
     GOOD ENOUGH FOR ALL BUT DRINKING WATER

PRESSURE RETURN LINE - PROVIDES PRESSURE FOR CLEAN OUT OF FILTER 1

BALL VALVE 5 - ACTIVATES PRESSURE RETURN LINE

TYPICAL FILTER BLOWOUT
WITH GARDEN HOSE TO
TAKE WATER OUT

WATER

TANK FILTER

3000 GAL TANK

PRESSURE RETURN LINE

BALL VALVE 5

BALL VALVE 4

PRESSURE GUAGE

HOSE BIB

12 VOLT DC PUMP

FILTER 3

FILTER 2

WATER TO FIXTURES

PRESSURE TANK

BALL VALVE 3

TANK "T"

BALL VALVE 2

FLEX HOSE

BALL VALVE 1

FILTER 1

43

"DIRTY WATER" CATCH SYSTEM

BALL VALVE 1 - SHUTS OFF TANK FROM SYSTEM

FILTER 1 - 50 MESH PROTECTS PUMP

FLEX HOSE - REQUIRED FOR VIBRATION OF PUMP

12 VOLT DC PUMP - PUSHES WATER INTO PRESSURE TANK

BALL VALVE 2 - ISOLATES PUMP FROM PRESSURE

TANK "T" - SPECIAL "T" TO ACCOMMODATE GAUGE AND HOSE BIB

BALL VALVE 3 - SHUTS OFF PRESSURE TANK FROM SYSTEM

PRESSURE TANK - PRESSURIZES SYSTEM

BALL VALVE 4 - ISOLATES FILTERS 2 & 3 FROM PRESSURE

FILTER 2 - 500 MESH STEPS UP TO 1000 MESH FILTER

FILTER 3 - 1000 MESH STEPS UP TO 5 MICRON FILTER
GOOD ENOUGH FOR ALL BUT DRINKING WATER

PRESSURE RETURN LINE - PROVIDES PRESSURE FOR CLEAN OUT OF FILTER 1

BALL VALVE 5 - ACTIVATES PRESSURE RETURN LINE

BALL VALVE 6 - ISOLATES FILTER 4 & DRINKING FILTER FROM PRESSURE

FILTER 4 - 5 MICRON TO PROTECT DRINKING FILTER

DRINKING FILTER - FILTERS OUT BACTERIA FOR DRINKING ALMOST ANY WATER

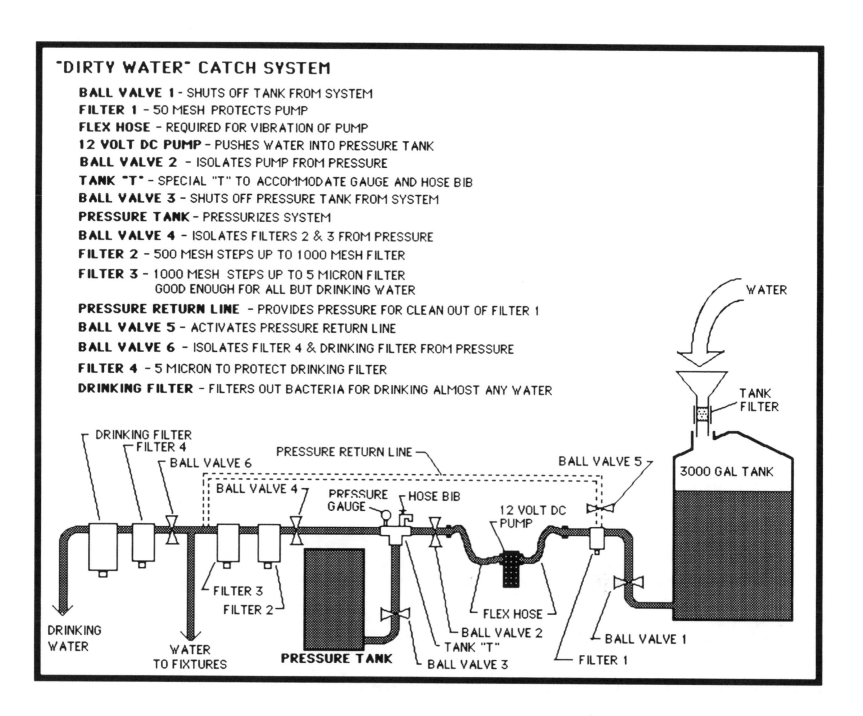

44

SOLAR SURVIVAL
RECOMMENDATIONS

This chapter has presented many options for the collection and distribution of domestic water. Various site conditions, climatic conditions, sizes of dwellings and budgets will further direct your choice. At this point, the best water supply for the least amount of money is achieved by collecting roof run-off only, from a slightly south pitched, (for cold climates) painted, Brai* or metal roof into a metal holding tank. Make the tank as large as you can afford - 3000 gallons for a 2 bedroom home. Use 2 tanks or one larger tank for more bedrooms. A small Sure Flow D.C. pump* with a filter installed before it is used to pump the water into a conventional pressure tank if the site doesn't allow gravity feed. The optimum use of the gravity concept would be for a large dwelling or community that steps up a hill. The upper roofs could collect water for a partially buried (to prevent freezing) holding tank that "gravity feeds" the rooms below. Filters and screens (as described on page 40-41) would still be required as water enters the tank. Decide if you have clear or dirty water and relate to the diagrams on pages 43 & 44. This will help you choose the number of filters you need. The special drinking water filter requires filters before it in the system to protect it.

Have your water tested to determine the need for a drinking water filter.

This would require no electricity or mechanical equipment for domestic water supply. The initial design and location of your Earthship relative to our "friends" gravity, rain and thermal mass would totally provide for domestic water needs.

*6 and 7 see Appendix, Chapter 2

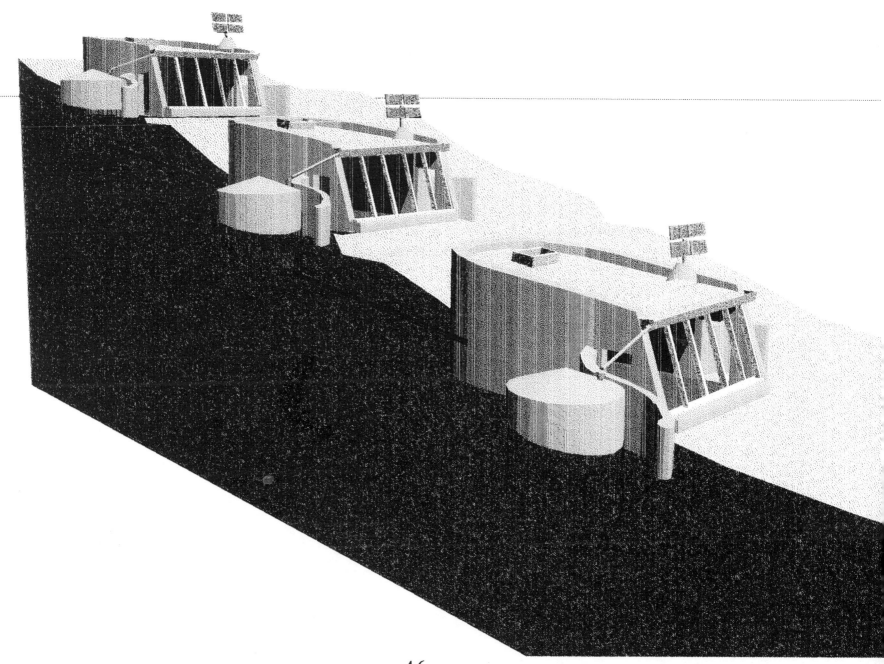

46

APPENDIX

Compost Toilets
MADE BY SUN-MAR
Order from SOLAR SURVIVAL ARCHITECTURE, P.O. Box 1041 Taos New Mexico, 87571 505 758-9870
See Chapter 3, p.63

Pumps
MADE BY SUREflo
Order from SOLAR SURVIVAL ARCHITECTURE, P.O. Box 1041 Taos, New Mexico, 87571 505 758-9870

1. #2088-044-135 6 amp pump delivers 3.6 gallons per minute. This is the pump used to pressurize the pressure tank in the systems recommended. It must have a 60 mesh filter before it to protect it. Don't ask it to pump higher than 8 feet.

2. This is a small booster pump for small time systems when a pressure tank is not being used. We have used it to service one sink in a studio without a pressure tank. Don't ask it to pump any higher than five feet.

3. DC well pumps
   FLOWLIGHT SOLAR POWER WORKSHOP

Rte. 1 Box 216
Espanola, NM 87532
1-505-753-9699

Pressure Tanks
Your local plumber or well driller can supply you with a conventional pressure tank. The larger you can afford, the better. We recommend 27 gallon draw down. This means you can take out 27 gallons before your pump is asked to work. If you have trouble, order one from SOLAR SURVIVAL ARCHITECTURE, P.O. Box 1041 Taos, New Mexico, 87571 505 758-9870

Paint coating for Brai roofing
Vindo Enamel by
LIVOS PAINT
1365 Rufina Circle
Sante Fe, New Mexico, 87501
505 988-9111

Low Flush Toilets
MADE BY SEALAND
Order from SOLAR SURVIVAL ARCHITECTURE, P.O. Box 1041 Taos, New Mexico, 87571 505 758-9870

Filters
Made by RUSCO
Clear, blow down filters

Order from your local plumber or
SOLAR SURVIVAL ARCHITECTURE
P.O. Box 1041, Taos, New Mexico 87571
505 758-9870
Blow down means you blow the filters out with water to clean them rather than constantly buying and replacing cartridges. These filters come in assorted meshes and micron densities.

Made by KATADYN
A drinking water filter, #HFK with built in spigot and #HFSK an in line filter

Tanks
Custom order a 3000 gallon galvanized steel tank with a 24" diameter manhole in the top with lid. Order a 6" diameter female threaded fitting at the top and a 1" diameter female threaded fitting at the bottom.

1. Local distributors of large galvanized tanks can be found in your area phone book. Freight is expensive on these. If you can find one close, it is better.

2. Tanks can be ordered from :
    SOLAR SURVIVAL ARCHITECTURE,
    P.O. Box 1041 Taos, New Mexico, 87571
    505 758-9870

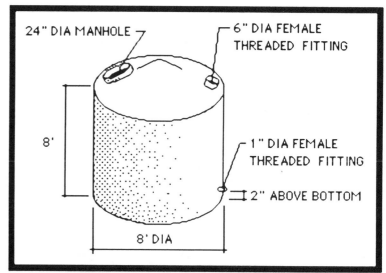

Submersible Pumps
1. FLOWLIGHT SOLAR POWER
    WORKSHOP
    Rte. 1 Box 216
    Espanola, NM 87532
    1-800-DC-SOLAR

2. PHOTOCOMM INC.
    Solar Electric Power Systems
    4419 E. Broadway
    Tucson, Arizona 85711
    (602) 327-8558

Annual Rainfall Information
1. National Weather Service-call for information in your state.

49

3. WASTE WATER

WITH THE GIVEN FACT THAT WATER IS BECOMING MORE AND MORE PRECIOUS DUE TO CARELESS CONSUMPTION, CONTAMINATION, AND SHEER NUMBERS OF HUMANS ON THE PLANET, WE MUST TOTALLY RETHINK WHAT WE DO WITH WASTE WATER. THE TRUTH IS THERE WILL BE NO SUCH THING AS *WASTE WATER*.

THIS CHAPTER WILL COVER METHODS AND CONCEPTS INVOLVED IN RECAPTURING AND REUSING ALL DOMESTIC WATER THAT IS USED IN THE DWELLING.

We are beginning to see on this planet that everything we "discard" has a value. Waste is not even a relevant issue with plants and animals. Everything is reused, transformed, or gives birth to something else as it dies. This is the frame of mind we must adopt as we decide what we do with our water after we have used it once.

Again we will start with an analysis of what we have been doing in our existing houses.

PRELIMINARY WASTE WATER ANALYSIS

BLACK WATER - TOILETS

Existing housing has two types of waste water - **black water** and **grey water**. Black water is from the toilets and needs treatment of some kind before it can be delivered back to the earth. Grey water is from everything else, sinks, tubs, showers, washing machines etc. If care is taken to use reasonably environmentally safe soaps, detergents etc, this water can (with designed control) be delivered immediately back into the earth both inside and outside the dwelling.

As discussed in the previous chapter, *using less* water makes both the effort of acquiring domestic water and dealing with "waste water" a smaller project. Thus **the first choice on how to deal with black water is to use compost toilets and therefore have no black water to deal with.**

Existing housing dumps all the black water (five gallons a flush) into the same sewage system or septic tank that the reusable grey water goes into. The result is a dozen times more black water to deal with than you had initially with just the toilet. Consequently we have massive sewage systems for even the smallest of towns. Individual homes have so much sewage that codes require they be on at least an acre of land for them to have their own septic system. This still requires soil percolation tests and EPA supervision to try to keep pollution of ground water to a minimum. In view of these facts, if you must have black water, **the first step toward dealing with it is to separate it from the grey water.** When black water is separate and low flush toilets that require a quart to a gallon of water are used, we are left with a much smaller amount of black water to deal with.

As the numbers of people continue to grow we must continue to reduce the "per capita black water volume". With black water down to a fraction of what a normal household would normally produce, the size and impact of the septic or sewage system can be greatly reduced. Septic tanks will be discussed later in the chapter.

GREY WATER

All other waste water can be reused immediately without treatment if a designed method is established. One rule of thumb is to **treat all the different sources of grey water (the tub/shower, the sink, the washing machine etc.) as separate entities so you won't have a large quantity of grey water in any one place.** A typical household gangs up all the grey water mixes it with the black water and has a big black water mess to deal with. The existing "solution" is to put it under the ground. Most of this "waste" that we put under ground is exactly what our plants (both inside and outside) would love to "eat". *We throw away nutrients for our plants in underground sewage systems. We do this in such a way that pollutes underground water tables. Then we buy manufactured "nutrients" for our plants which aren't as good as what we threw away.* This is modern day waste water technology.

The Kitchen Sink

In one of my early experimental Earthships I drained my kitchen sink in to its' own individual *inside* planter. I put a little ten inch tall $2.98 split leaf philodendron in the planter. Within a couple of years the plant became a fifteen foot tall tree with an 8" diameter trunk with seed pods and other weird things I have never seen on a philodendron before. This plant is so healthy and strong from the "food" produced by the kitchen sink that no bug or disease could touch it . It is a *being*.

The kitchen sink in a normal household probably swallows everything from Drano to Clorox to turpentine. **It is also the collector of a tremendous amount of organic matter.** The first step here is to stop putting anything down your kitchen sink that you know would be harmful to plants. Garbage disposals (in addition to increasing your electrical demand) allow the potential for all kinds of things to be ground up and washed down the drain. They should be not be used in an Earthship with a grey water system. Most dish soaps are designed to be good for your hands so, consequently, they are also ok for plants. Small amounts of dish soap mixed with water as a spray deters inside planting pests such as white flies. However, the key to dealing with pests is to have strong healthy plants fed by grey water. *No bug would even think about bothering my philodendron*

All food stuffs, drinkable liquids, and dish water are welcome food for a kitchen sink planter. Specific methods of developing a kitchen sink planter will be discussed later. The issue here is that **the kitchen sink be dealt with as a producer of strong plant food and individually drained into its own planter.** There is no need for vents and traps as the building codes demand. This is true because vents and traps are for blocking and venting sewer gases - a simple open drain sink into a planter *has*

no gas . In most cases we have still had to put them in even though they are not needed because *the Code said so*. However, we are currently working on a research and development project involving several buildings which will be allowed to pursue these ideas with code variances for a limited time. The result here will be a method of dealing with kitchen sink "waste" water that is cheaper than conventional methods, that makes good food for plants, and that results in less sewage for *whatever* system to deal with.

Bathroom Sinks

Conventional use of bathroom sinks involves things like shaving for ten minutes with the water running which is simply a waste of water. Even with this careless use, the bathroom sink is still a minor water and nutrient producer with less chance for strange things to be poured down it than a kitchen sink. Much of the same information regarding kitchen sinks is also true for bathroom sinks with respect to what you should and should not put down them if you want to use them for watering a planter. They are normally trapped and vented and drained into a sewage or septic system which is a waste of some perfectly good grey water that could very easily be used for watering plants. Bathroom sinks could be an easy contributor to indoor plant watering.

Showers and Tubs

Conventional tubs and showers are major producers of large volumes of water. This large volume of water is usually mixed right in with the black water and is one of the major reasons we have so much raw sewage to deal with in conventional housing. As discussed in Chapter Two, this volume can and should be cut way down, however the potential volume of water here usually requires that the grey water be taken to an outside planter. The various soaps and shampoos are not harmful (if anything, helpful) to plants and they love the oils and grime that you wash off of your body. Whereas showers and tubs present a major <u>burden</u> on conventional sewage and septic systems, they could be a major <u>contributor</u> to the watering and nurturing of outside landscaping.

Washing Machines

Normally, washing machines are a serious source of some of the weirder water produced by a household because of bleaches, strong detergents etc. In a normal septic system, these liquids are responsible for seriously retarding if not destroying the effect of the anaerobic process that is supposed to take place in a septic tank. Some of the liquids we put down our drains actually kill the bacteria that are supposed to be working. The result is that the septic system does not produce a sludge that is welcomed back to the earth. It produces a vile sludge that is not welcomed anywhere. Washing machines are normally vented and trapped and are a major contributor to the volume of a septic system. They could, however, be open drained into a controlled exterior grey water planting area. This assumes that environmentally safe detergents and bleaches are used.

Dishwashers

Dishwashers use electricity and a large volume of water both hot and cold. The result is taxing on four systems - electrical, sewage, water, and hot water. This raises a question - is a dish washer worth it? They can be made to work on all these systems but they will make every system a bit more expensive to put into operation. *There are differing opinions on whether a dishwasher uses more water or not. If the dishwashing person is conscious of his/her water use, he/she could easily use less water than the machine. This, in addition to their electrical demand, makes this one of the items to consider dropping from your appliance list.* If a dishwasher is incorporated into an Earthship design it should be used only occasionally if you really want to sail without effort and with minimal initial investment in an Earthship. The best advice is to not use a dishwashing machine.

All of this grey water together is a significant amount even if one is being conservative with the use of water. **Why do we throw this water away?** Not only is it water, it contains <u>free nutrients</u> for our plants. Throwing it away creates volume problems for our various "modern" sewage systems. Then we have to use <u>more</u> water to water our plants both inside and outside. Also it costs more money to throw it away than to <u>use</u> it. How did this happen?

THE BASICS OF BLACK AND GREY WATER SYSTEMS

As with the other chapters, we will not cover ground in the following explanations that is common knowledge to conventional plumbers and various technicians or that is already available in various plumbing manuals etc. We are attempting to put forth concepts and methods that are here-to-fore little understood and little known (if known at all) for dealing with black and grey water. The actual execution of these methods involves nothing that is not already commonly practiced by conventional plumbers, builders etc.

COMPOST TOILETS

There are two types of compost toilets. The most simple and least expensive is the self-contained unit that composts right where it sets. It is vented like a stove. You add peat moss daily to help "prime the pump" for the composting process.

You take a tray of peat moss material out every month. <u>This material can be put right on the ground surface.</u> The new models (see Appendix, Chapter 3) work very well and don't smell. However, as insurance, always put them in their own compartment with a door and an operable skylight (see Chapter 8 for gravity operated skylights). If you think of this unit as an isolated, vented, "indoor outhouse" you won't be disappointed. They cost about $1200 and almost nothing to install.

There are also flush type compost toilets that flush like an airplane toilet with a pedal. They flush into a compost unit placed below the dwelling. (This composting unit also requires the addition of peat moss daily if you are home and using it and emptying the tray of "soil" monthly.) The fact that it is not in the living space is attractive to many people. It costs about $1400 for the unit itself, plus $1000 to install and requires a composting space below the dwelling. One compost unit will handle two toilets with proper maintenance. We have combined the compost room with the battery room (discussed in Chapter 1) and this works quite well.

The appendix to Chapter Three presents information on how to acquire compost toilets and how to review their performance before you purchase one. This remains the first choice as to how to deal with black water - **don't have any in the first place.** This is the least expensive and most environmentally appropriate way to go. If (for whatever reason) you can't go this way then your best choice is to use a septic tank for black water only.

SEPTIC TANKS

If your toilet(s) is the only thing going into your septic tank, (and it should be) your septic tank and drain field can be very small even with a conventional "waste flush" toilet. With a low flush toilet, the septic tank can be even smaller. Since this concept (like most environmentally appropriate issues) is not even considered in the "real" world, there are no small septic tanks on the market and chances are the codes wouldn't let you use one anyway. Building codes determine the size of a septic tank based on the size of the house. They also require a minimum lot size - (usually) an acre for a septic system. These code requirements are based on the following:

1. Standard wasteful consumption of water by most households.
2. The common practice of mixing useful grey water with black water.
3. The very existence of black water.
4. The common practice of dumping toxic fluids "down the drain".

These are considered "givens" by the building codes.There is no way for the codes to relate to the person who has only a minimal amount of black water to deal with and who uses grey water systems. Common practice would therefore be to make you use a typical 1000 gallon septic tank with a forty foot drain field on one acre of land to the tune of $1500 to $2000 not to mention the fact that you have to have enough land to accommodate it. These code dilemmas will be discussed further in another chapter. Suffice it to say for now that we are talking here about "OUTLAW SEPTIC TANKS" that break code only because code is not evolved enough to apply.

The basic idea of a septic tank is to have an underground tank (in this case a very small one) that has an inlet and an outlet. The inlet is the black water coming from your dwelling in a 3" plastic ABS pipe sloped at 1/4" per foot. The outlet is simply the same size pipe with the same slope installed on the other side of the tank. This pipe however, is 2" lower. The pipes have a sweeping "T" on the ends to direct the water down and to protect the pipes from floating debris should the water level get that high.

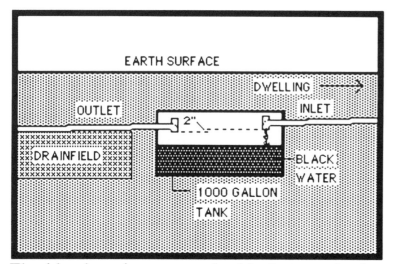

EARTH SURFACE

DWELLING →

OUTLET   INLET

2"

DRAINFIELD

BLACK WATER

1000 GALLON TANK

The idea here is to store the black water in the tank for a period of time (as long as it takes to fill up the tank). This allows all the solids and paper to turn into a thicker liquid sludge and begin an anaerobic process with natural bacteria. When the tank fills up with this sludge the liquid begins to move out the lower pipe and into a drainfield for distribution back to the soil. Normally the drainfield, like the tank, is sized very large (40' or more) due to the tremendous volume caused by the ridiculous practice of mixing black water with immediately reusable grey water.

Except for the ridiculous volume, this was a reasonably sound concept before Drano, Clorox, turpentine and other things began to be poured down our drains. These liquids kill the natural bacteria which turns the sludge into a natural earth product welcomed back into the soil. So what we end up with here is a really vile sludge not welcomed in the earth or anywhere else. Code is designed to make sure this bad stuff is kept under ground where the nice humans are safe from it. It is already a given in most rural areas that the first level of water is contaminated by septic systems, consequently wells all have to go much deeper (at greater expense) to second water. It is the massive **volume** and the Drano, etc. that makes septic systems such a problem. A simple little one or two toilet black water septic tank with no harmful fluids flushed down would not require a full acre of land and the fluids would be welcomed back to the land as a natural product.

Outlaw Septic I

This is simply a small dome made of aluminum cans set on a typical concrete slab. Chapter 9 covers the process of making domes, vaults, etc. out of aluminum cans. For one low-flush toilet the tank only needs to be about 4'-6" in diameter on the inside. For two toilets make it 5'-0" in diameter. The first step is to pour a conventional concrete slab about 4'-6" below where your outlet is coming out of your dwelling. This should be about ten feet from the house. The slab should be 5'-6" (or 6'-0" for the larger size) in diameter to allow for the thickness of the aluminum cans. It should have conventional re-mesh or structural fibers (consult a local contractor) for reinforcement.

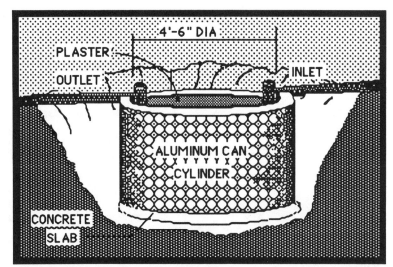

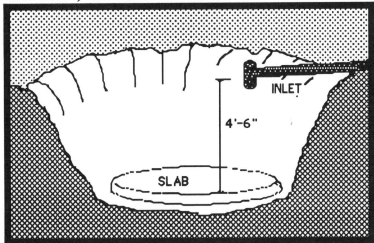

Lay up a can masonry cylinder about 4'-0" tall. (see Chapter 9).

At this point bring in your inlet and outlet. Make sure the outlet is 2" below the inlet and that both have 1/4" per foot slopes. Lock them in with a few more courses of cans to make sure they will not move now that you have them positioned. These cans can be slightly pulled in toward the center to begin the "cone" roof of the tank.

Now you are ready to plaster the inside so the tank will hold water. First a scratch coat then a smooth troweled coat of conventional hard plaster mix. The formula for this is one part cement to three parts plaster sand with water as necessary.

Next you begin laying the cone all the way up by pulling the cans in toward the center about 1/2" per course. The cone is tapered in to a 2'-0" diameter opening at the top which is then covered with a concrete lid made by pouring some concrete out of a wheel barrow over a 2'-0" circle of 6x6 reinforcing mesh and shaping it by hand or with a trowel into the desired circle. This disc should be a little larger than the opening so it can rest on the tapering can wall of the cone.

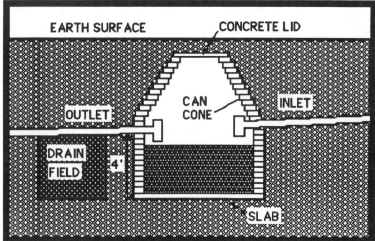

The lid will facilitate clean out which is a typical feature of all septic tanks although seldom ever needed in a "toilet only" septic tank. This lid can be buried under about 6" to 8" of soil.

This septic tank like all septic tanks has a drain field to distribute the processed fluid back into the earth. The difference here is that instead of a forty foot drain field you only need about a ten or twelve foot drain field. The drain field should be a trench about four feet deeper than the position at which the outlet leaves the septic tank and twelve to fourteen feet long. Fill the trench up with typical drainage rock which is 2" to 8" in

diameter. Attach a ten or twelve foot length of 3" drainage pipe to the outlet with a plastic couple. The drainage pipe has two sets of holes that are to be placed down toward the rock.

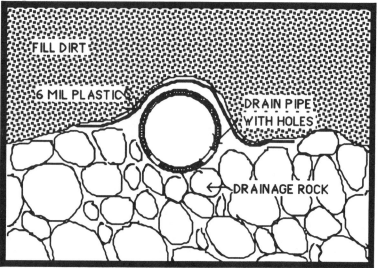

A layer of 6 mil plastic is usually placed over this to keep backfill dirt from seeping down into the gravel. This drain field is done exactly like that for a conventional septic tank if you wish to consult a local septic tank contractor. It is simply much shorter due to the fact that you are dealing with a significantly smaller volume of liquid.

The only real difference between this septic system and a conventional septic system is size and consequently cost. This method enables the home owner him/herself to install the septic system as opposed to having to pay a septic tank contractor to install his smallest system (to the tune of about $2000) which is much larger than you need for just a toilet. This system is absolutely to code. It is just on a smaller scale. A reasonable inspector should allow this system if he will allow the rest of your fixtures to be on their own grey water system.

Outlaw Septic II

This system is one step above an outhouse. It simply allows you to have your toilet inside. The little bit of water used in a low flush toilet helps to create a sludge as opposed to just having a stack of shit like outhouses do. *Don't even ask an inspector to approve of this system.* This design is for more rural areas where inspection is not an issue. It is, however, a great way to get a flush toilet working on a minimum budget. I have used it many times. It is both easy and economical and can be installed in one afternoon. If used only for a low-flush toilet, it is perfectly harmless to the underground. A concentrated accumulation of human shit will simply turn into rich soil under ground if it is not carried all over the place with huge volumes of water, Drano and paint thinner, etc. This system is for a toilet (preferably low-flush) only. All other grey water should be dealt with separately.

The 3" inlet from the dwelling is conventional from the toilet. In this design, the tank and drainfield are the same thing. **This is possible only if the low flush toilet is the only fixture emptying into the system.** Dig a hole with a backhoe about eight to ten feet deeper than the position of the outlet coming from the dwelling. This hole should be about eight feet square. Collect about six or eight old discarded **backhoe tires.** Lay one on the leveled bottom of the hole and fill loose dirt around it lightly tamping the dirt as you fill.

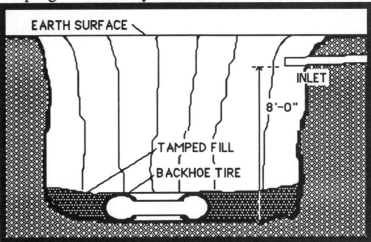

Now add another tire and repeat the process all the way up to your inlet.

If you do not come out exactly where your inlet (with its appropriate slope) will lay on the last tire, make up the difference with rocks. Rocks will also have to be used to circle the top course of tires in order to incorporate the 3" plastic inlet thus leaving a level circle to receive the concrete lid.

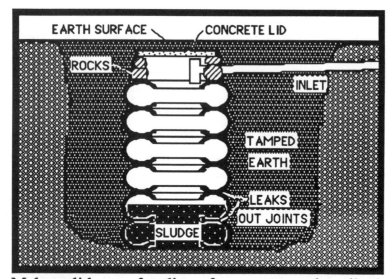

EARTH SURFACE — CONCRETE LID

ROCKS

INLET

TAMPED EARTH

LEAKS OUT JOINTS

SLUDGE

Make a lid out of a disc of concrete as described before in Outlaw Septic Tank I and install it over the circle of rocks. Bury this lid only about 6" deep and you have a septic tank/outhouse with the stool inside. In this case what little bit of sludge there is will penetrate the joints between the tires and return to the earth immediately around the unit. Due to the small amount of water content which creates a sludge, one toilet will never fill a drainfield/tank combination like this. The price is about $300 max. and you can begin flushing.

GREY WATER
Kitchen Sinks
The kitchen sink gets used every day and has the potential for producing significant amounts of highly nutritious grey water. The sink can be simply elbowed and clear drained without a trap

or a vent into a nearby planter. The pipe going to the planter should be 2" ABS drain pipe with 1/4" per foot slope.

Since Earthships are so conducive to the interior growing of plants the planter can be located almost anywhere. Obviously more options are available in a multilevel Earthship than in a dwelling all on one level. Following is an example of an interior planter positioned to receive kitchen sink grey water.

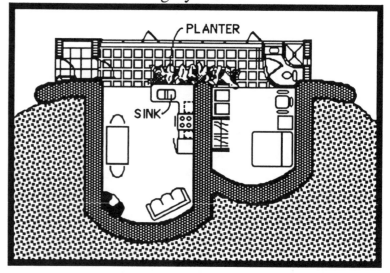

PLANTER

SINK

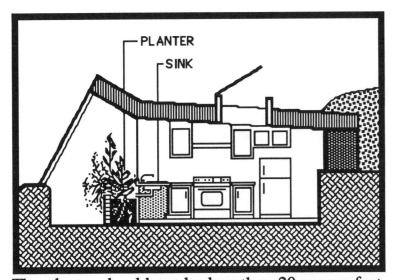

PLANTER

SINK

The planter should not be less than 20 square feet in surface area with a foot of top soil and a foot of gravel beneath the top soil. The pipe should be open to the planter so the water *falls* a few inches into the planter and is then irrigated around in it via dirt trenches. Do not have the pipe go under the ground into the soil of the planter. This will make it so you need a trap as you will be trapping grey water gases. Sometimes the drain pipe is split so it will run part way down both directions of the planter to further distribute the water before it falls to the dirt.

Kitchen sinks are best for watering small trees and large plants. Be prepared for anything you plant in this planter to get *very large*. Small ground cover type plants should not be used alone here as they are not large enough to absorb the water whereas larger plants (trees, grapevines etc.) basically suck up the water as opposed to having it just stand or be absorbed into the planter soil. The success of this kind of high volume grey water planter (especially an inside one) is dependent on having a large hungry plant (or plants) to take all the nutrient rich water, quickly suck it up into limbs and branches and give it back to you as foliage, blooms and beauty. The planter also wants to be in direct sun as this will help create the need for the water.

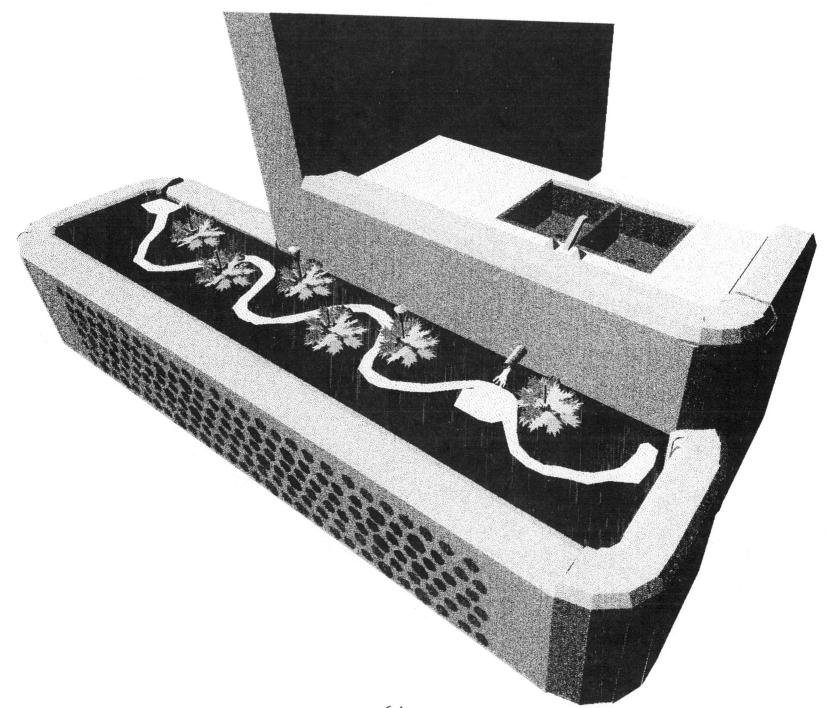

64

Bathroom Sinks

The amount of water a bathroom sink produces is much less both in volume and nutrients than a kitchen sink. You can therefore take it into almost any sized planter nearby or far away, inside or outside. You will still have to water this planter with an auxiliary water source as there is just not enough water produced by a bathroom sink to take the full load of any planter unless it is quite small- like four square feet. Once you have established a bathroom sink as a grey water supply for any planter, you can always use that sink faucet specifically for running water down the drain and watering the planter whether you are using the sink or not. This is one of the beauties of grey water systems. You are killing two birds with one stone. You don't have to put a watering hose bib in the planter because the bathroom sink (or whatever sink) is available for the sole purpose of watering the planter if need be. You are therefore saving on the installation and duplication of plumbing faucets and fixtures.

The size and slope of the pipe are the same as that described for the kitchen sink. Vents and traps are not necessary again as long as you provide an actual fall of water from an open pipe for at least four inches.

Since bathroom sinks are not usually as high as kitchen sinks, achieving a fall from the drain pipe is not always possible. In this case a mini drain field is necessary. The 2" ABS pipe comes out of the sink and lays in a bed of gravel just under the surface of the planter (4" to 6"). The pipe is drilled on both sides of the bottom with weep holes and capped on the end. This is to assure water distribution through the weep holes rather than the end.

Other than the reuse of water and the savings on plumbing fixtures another beauty of grey water systems is that you save time. You are watering you planter while you are brushing your teeth as opposed to brushing your teeth and then watering your planter. **Multiple results from one action is a way of natural phenomenon of the planet and the universe.** It is a sign of broader awareness as opposed to the single-mindedness of mice and some men.

Since the bathroom sinks usually do not handle near the volume of liquids that a kitchen sink does, nor do they have as many nutrients, they can be drained without vents and traps into almost any nearby planter. They may not even provide enough water for that planter. The point is that they will not be contributing to an under ground or municipal sewer load. Also watch what kind of mouthwash you use. Some of them may not be good for plants!

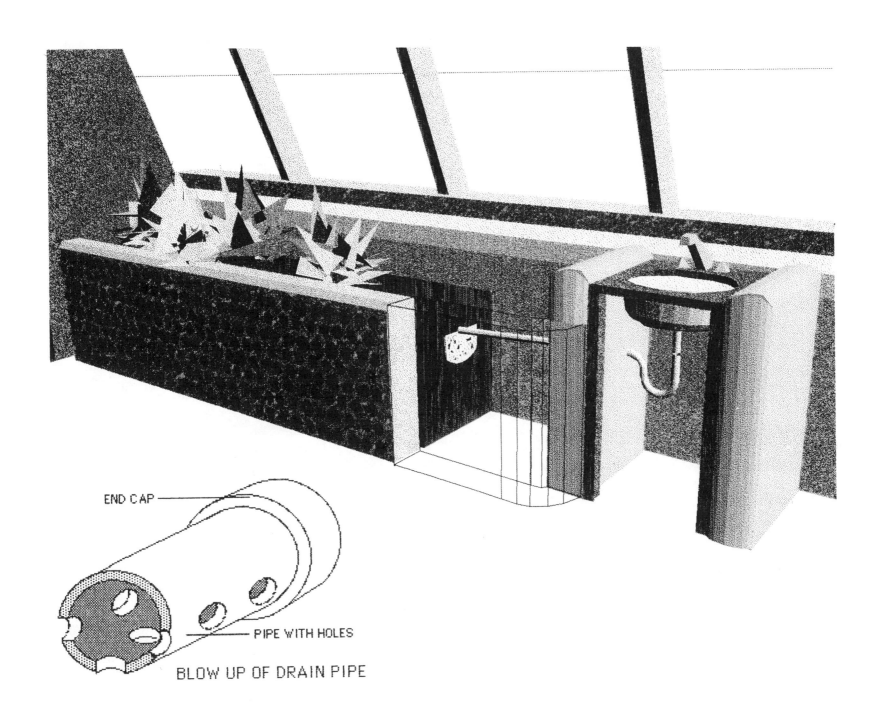

END CAP

PIPE WITH HOLES

BLOW UP OF DRAIN PIPE

Showers and Tubs

Here the volume of water is too large to keep inside unless you have an unusually large planting area. Typically tubs and showers should be detailed just like sinks with respect to pipe size and slope but they must go outside to a grey water bed of eighty square feet or more depending on the number of people using the shower or tub. A rule of thumb is that if you see standing water, your bed is not large enough. This grey water bed can be irrigated with little pathways in the dirt to carry the water to all parts of the bed. Plant things that like a lot of water such as willows, roses, or trees.

In a situation where the dwellings may be close together, the grey water bed will have to be contained in an open tank of some kind to assure that it does not run into someone else's property or terrain. This open tank can be a simple galvanized cattle watering tank or anything similar. In this situation the tank should be filled with 8" of gravel on the bottom then filled the rest of the way with soil. The quality of the soil is not too important because after you run your bath water through it for a year or so it is going to be rich. Again be sure to let the water fall clear of piping for at least 4" to avoid trapping gases or smells in your open unvented pipe.

Except for the codes, there is again no reason to vent or trap a tub or shower drain that goes outside into a grey water bed. In some cases where dwellings are close together these beds would have to be contained as described above. The issue here is that **grey water from tubs and showers be taken outside the dwelling and treated separately from everything else as their volume of water is enough for any one given spot.** Irrigation, i.e. good distribution of this water is important.

Washing Machines

Washing machines should be treated very similarly to showers and tubs. They can go into their own large grey water bed. However it is a good idea to distribute all of this free rich water to different parts of your landscaping if possible. A reason for keeping washing machines separate is that some detergents and/or bleaches you may use could be a little harsh for the plants you have planted in your bath greywater bed. It is important to remember, especially with these larger volume grey water beds, that you design, locate and plant them so they work for you and your landscaping. We are not talking about just dumping water on to the surface of the ground. We are talking about controlled and designed reuse of nutrient rich water carefully integrated in to a landscaping program.

Other Things

Floor drains, Laundry sinks, and other plumbing fixtures all fall into one of the previous categories as far as the method of drainage. The idea of separation of fixtures cannot be carried too far as this distributes the grey water to many places.

The overall effects of grey water systems are significant.

1 They reduce the cost of the building in that they ELIMINATE the need for a large commercial septic system.

2 They further reduce the cost of the building in that they ELIMINATE the need for vents traps and some plant watering SYSTEMS.

3 They provide NUTRIENTS to the landscaping both inside and out that would otherwise have to be bought and added to the soil. Commercial fertilizers often mix these nutrients with harmful chemicals.

4 They allow watering of household plants and outdoor landscaping to occur within the DAILY ROUTINE of the home owner thus saving time and/or REDUCING the need for an expensive automatic watering system.

5 They REUSE water thus greatly reducing each individual home owners personal consumption of water. *This is perhaps the most significant effect of grey water systems.*

OUR RECOMMENDATIONS

1. Use a self contained compost toilet in its own little room with a gravity operated skylight.

2. Drain your kitchen sink into a large hungry indoor planter positioned so you will get some enjoyment out of the large plants that will grow there.

3. Drain all bathroom sinks into the nearest planter to avoid piping. If your home has different levels, make the planters lower to avoid the necessity of a mini drain field.

4. Don't use a dishwasher.

5. Drain tubs and showers into well distributed exterior landscaping. Plant a tree here.

6. Drain washing machines into well distributed exterior landscaping. Plant a tree here

APPENDIX

Compost Toilets
MADE BY SUN-MAR
Order from SOLAR SURVIVAL ARCHITECTURE, P.O. Box 1041, Taos, New Mexico, 87571 505 758-9870

Sun-Mar makes four models of toilets. Two of these use electricity and therefore are not considered here. The other two do require the possible use of a small DC fan. This depends on the installation, location and use. The N.E. works for one to three people and is a unit that requires no plumbing. Install it in a small well vented room of its own like an enclosed toilet stall with an operable skylight above.(See Chapter 8 on Gravity Skylights). The WCM-N.E. is basically the same unit only it is remote from the bathroom and requires a SEALAND lowflush toilet. The toilet flushes like an air plane toilet and requires no vent. The remote WCM however does require a straight up 4" vent from its remote location. Three inch typical ABS plastic sewer pipe at 1/4" per foot slope connects the toilet to the composting unit. With the plumbing, the toilet and the composting unit, this is a much more expensive solution. However, because it is more like a conventional toilet, many prefer it.

Low Flush Toilets
MADE BY SEALAND
Order from SOLAR SURVIVAL ARCHITECTURE, P.O. Box 1041, Taos, New Mexico, 87571 505 758-9870

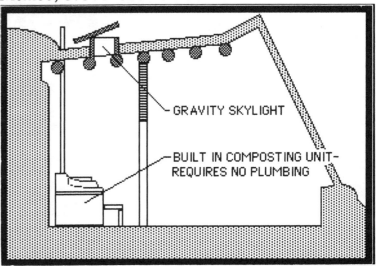

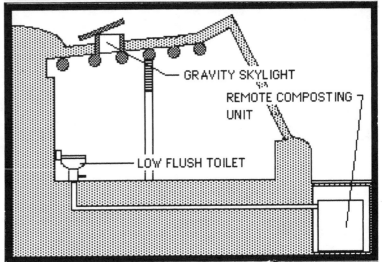

See photo next page

71

4. HOT WATER
S Y S T E M S

WE HAVE GROWN ACCUSTOMED TO THE AVAILABILITY OF ALL THE HOT WATER WE CAN USE. MAYBE IT IS TIME TO LOOK AT THE REALITY OF HOW MUCH HOT WATER WE *NEED*. THE EARTHSHIP VOLUMES ARE AIMED AT SIMPLE, COMFORTABLE SURVIVAL NOT LUXURIOUS AMERICAN DECADENCE. THERE ARE MANY WAYS TO GET ENDLESS AMOUNTS OF HOT WATER FOR DOMESTIC PURPOSES. THERE ARE BUT A FEW THAT ARE BOTH ECONOMICAL AND APPROPRIATE WHEN ONE CONSIDERS THE NUMBERS OF PEOPLE AND THE CURRENT CONDITION OF THE PLANET IN TERMS OF EXTRACTED ENERGY. THEREFORE, WE WILL ONLY DISCUSS THE FEW SIMPLE METHODS OF OBTAINING HOT WATER THAT, AFTER TWENTY YEARS OF RESEARCH IN SELF-SUFFICIENT LIVING, STILL LOOK FEASIBLE BOTH ECONOMICALLY AND ECOLOGICALLY. AS WITH THE PREVIOUS CHAPTERS, WE WILL FIRST PRESENT A METHOD OF <u>FREE</u> HOT WATER PRODUCTION WHICH REQUIRES SOME PERSONAL CHANGES OF HABIT AND ATTITUDE, THEN A METHOD THAT COMES A LITTLE CLOSER TO WHAT WE ARE ACCUSTOMED TO BUT IS THE LESSER OF THE EVILS, SO TO SPEAK. AS FOR ALL THE OTHER METHODS OF OBTAINING ENDLESS AMOUNTS OF HOT WATER, THERE ARE OTHER BOOKS.

The only problem with acquiring solar hot water in the sun belt areas is *when* we need it. If we can adjust our lives to the rhythms of the natural phenomena, our problems would be few. Solar hot water is very easy to produce. It is, however, more difficult and more expensive to have *on hand* during the night or during cloudy days. It follows that solar hot water in predominantly cloudy areas is next to impossible and very expensive if it is possible at all. Therefore, we must also explore the most efficient methods of producing hot water with fossil fuels.

As with all the other household systems, our current personal requirements must be examined. The two factors involved in hot water (as well as all the other systems) are: your level of consciousness with regard to the rest of the beings on the planet and/or your level of wealth or buying power with *disregard* to the rest of the beings on the planet. For a while yet, you will be able to buy the amount of fuel you need to get as much hot water as you want, but who knows how long this will last? Will it mean the end of the last wilderness areas on the planet to get at the oil? Then again, maybe it will just mean blowing away a few Arabs and losing a few thousand American youths in the process. Having dealt with the intertwined, interrelated aspect of all systems of independent living for twenty years, I do have something to say besides the moralistic fanatical

meanderings above on the subject of hot water. First lets look at how you get hot water in conventional housing.

PRELIMINARY HOT WATER ANALYSIS

Conventionally, we heat water in a tank with gas or electricity. We keep it hot and available all day and night whether we are home or not. Many homes also circulate this hot water for instant availability at the tap. Until recently the tanks that we heated up and stored our hot water in were not very well insulated. With the continuing various "alarms" relative to the unstable situation of earth energy for human consumption, we have made the *major leap* to better insulating our hot water tanks. This is not enough.

An average 75 gallon gas or electric hot water heater costs from two to five hundred dollars. This will provide hot water for a two, maybe three bedroom home. Sometimes someone may have to wait for the hot water heater to recover in order to take a shower. Operation of this hot water heater will cost from $40 to $60 a month to keep water hot depending on the current cost of gas and electricity. After a year, your hot water heater has cost you a thousand dollars and still counting - assuming gas or electricity has not doubled in price and is still available throughout the various military, economic and ecological crises we are looking at. In view of these facts lets look at a few different methods of obtaining hot water beginning with the simplest, most economical and easiest.

ALTERNATIVE OPTIONS
FOR THE FANATIC

Move to the sun belt (southwest) and use a solar batch heater. This will only give you hot water on sunny days (which is 90% of the time in the southwest) and it will be late morning before you get it. In the winter months you may only get one batch (70 gallons) a day on sunny days and in the summer you will get two batches. You will have hot water way up into the night so you are only without hot water in the early morning and on cloudy days. A batch heater can cost $1000 to $2000 depending on volume and from then on it is totally free and will last you the rest of your life. You are dependent on no fossil fuels of any kind and the only price is that you conform to the performance of the heater with your use of hot water. **All aspects of survival become very easy when we allow <u>ourselves</u> to follow the phenomenon rather than forcing phenomena to follow us.** There is nothing like sitting in a tub of scalding hot water knowing it was free for both you and the planet. In a large Earthship, solar batch heaters could be used over every bathroom to avoid the pumping and circulation of hot water throughout the home.

If you want to have hot water the next morning bright and early and you have a little more money to spend, drain your batch heater into a super-insulated storage tank and pump it to the tap. This obviously involves more equipment and more money and a slight bit of solar electricity, but, except for those few times (in the southwest) when there are several cloudy days in a row, you would have hot or very warm water 95% of the time.

FOR THE ENERGY CONSCIOUS

If you can't move to the sun belt and there is not enough sun where you live to make a solar batch heater practical, then a gas demand heater (these have been used in Europe for years) is the answer. These heaters heat the water in a coil as it is called for. Only a pilot burns until you turn on the tap. Then there is a burst of flame and the water is passed thru the flame in a copper coil. The flame remains on, heating the water in the coil as long as you have the tap on. You never run out of hot water and you don't waste fuel keeping a tank full of hot water when you are not at home or not using it. You only heat what you are immediately using and then the unit is off. There are many brands of these "on demand" heaters but the Paloma (see Appendix, Chapter 4) is, so far, the most trouble free (and most expensive) I have found. The others cost less but you spend more than the difference very soon in parts, replacements, adjustments etc. This is a very simple concept in hot water heating and it doesn't involve any pumps, tanks, etc. They do, however, require that the water pass through a good in-line filter *before* the hot water heater as the coils can get clogged with particles or burnt off impurities in the water. The filter type can be determined by a water test. See your local plumber for information on how and where to get your water tested. Your plumber can usually then sell you the filter you need. (See Appendix, Chapter 4).

These heaters cost in the neighborhood of $800 and will work for a one bathroom home. Two bathrooms require two heaters. Generally speaking, they cost about fifteen dollars a month to operate in a one bathroom home with 1991 gas prices. They work off of propane or natural gas. There are various sizes, a smaller one for an efficiency apartment or a single person and a larger size for more people or bathrooms. However, in a large home with two or three bathrooms, the best use of these heaters is to put a medium sized one at each bathroom as the larger units (sized for more output) use more gas. Another factor here is the inefficiency (both in terms of water and energy) and the wait when the hot water heater is not close to the fixtures it services. In very large homes the use of an "on demand " heater <u>near</u> each bathroom and maybe a shared one for kitchen and utility is the best way to avoid a *hot water system* with pumps, circulation, storage and the use of electricity.

THE COMBO

For the best of both worlds, a combination solar batch heater and demand heater can work very well. There are many levels of execution of this combination. The most simple being a solar batch heater independent of the demand heater with a valve to choose one or the other depending on the availability of the solar hot water. This is obviously more expensive than one or the other but it gives you the security of hot water whenever you want it and the advantage of *free hot water* when it is available. In the sun belt this can cut the hot water heating expense by 75% as you only use gas when there is no sun or in early morning.

There is also the more complicated possibility of a solar batch heater and insulated storage tank used separately or in conjunction with a demand heater. The batch heater (or warmed water in the storage tank) can be used as a preheater for the demand heater thus enabling you to use less gas to heat the water already warmed by the batch heater as opposed to heating cold water straight from a well. This situation calls for a different brand of demand heater - the Aquastar - which allows the already warmed water to use less gas to take it the rest of the way up to what you would call hot. The Paloma does not have this feature. It takes the same amount of gas no matter what the temperature of the water coming through.

OTHER OPTIONS

There is an intense solar heater that is a step up from a custom batch heater - a convection heat storage unit.* It is a plate type intense collector with a built-in insulated tank. This unit uses convection (the movement of hot water upward) to move the water from heater to tank. Neither pumps nor electricity are necessary. This unit will work where a batch heater won't because the intense collector heats a small amount of water that is constantly rising to the tank. Obviously a smaller amount of water is easier to heat with less sun. This unit is expensive but it is one of the few alternatives in areas outside the "sunbelt" if solar hot water is desired. There is also a relatively new device called the Copper Cricket* which can heat the water in your existing hot water heater. It costs over $2000 plus some installation expenses. It works without any pumps or electricity and is also a recommended alternative.

There are many intense plate and tube collectors (see Appendix, Chapter 4) on the market which heat smaller amounts of water faster and hotter. These require an insulated storage tank to store the water which is pumped with electricity to the tap from the storage tank. These are *systems* which require electricity and they are expensive both in terms of materials and installation as they have many components.

The best *tank* gas hot water heater on the market is the "Nautilus". This unit has the combustion component submerged in the water rather than an open flame under the unit as a conventional *tank* gas hot water heater does. This obviously reduces the amount of energy that is wasted, however, this unit still uses the old concept of heating a tank of water and keeping it hot. They do not supply an endless quantity of hot water as a demand unit does but they have an impressive recovery time. If you want to stay with the conventional tank hot water heater, this is the way to go.

THE BOTTOM LINE

1. Re-evaluate your use of hot water in conjunction with your budget and your environmental conscience.
2. Avoid a *system* and the use of electricity to provide or circulate hot water.
3. Be willing to spend more money now for less money and more security later.
4. If you are unable to adapt to the availability of the sun for hot water production at this point in your life and are on a limited

*1 see Appendix, Chapter 4

budget, use a Paloma "on demand" hot water heater.

5. If you can adjust your lifestyle, are on a limited budget and want to be free, use a solar batch heater.

6. If you can adjust your life-style and are not on such a tight budget, use a solar batch heater with a storage tank or in combination with an "on demand" heater.

7. Large home and tight budget = two or more "on demand" heaters.

8. Large home and loose budget = combo of "on demand" heaters and solar batch heaters strategically placed.

9. Loose budget/fanatic/true believer in the sun belt = solar batch heater (or heaters) with super-insulated storage tank (or tanks).

10. Loose budget/fanatic/true believer outside the sun belt = convection heater storage unit.

THE BASICS OF HOT WATER DEVICES

This section will explain the basic function and assembly of the methods of obtaining hot water described above.

SOLAR BATCH HEATERS

The simplest, low-tech and maintenance-free method of obtaining hot water anywhere near the sun-belt is a solar batch heater. Batch heaters are called such because they are both the heater and the storage tank for a "batch" of hot water. The tank should to be as large as possible to hold as much water as possible. The tank also has to be relatively thin so it will get the water hot enough fast enough. Other factors of size are the fact that tempered glass will have to cover the unit and since it is expensive, you don't want to have to use too large a piece (or pieces) of glass. Also, the unit is usually integrated into the profile and warmth of your Earthship in some way so it shouldn't be too tall, creating a profile of it's own. Batch heaters are seldom pressurized with your water system so they depend on gravity flow to deliver the water. A batch heater is basically a thin rectalinear tank with glass in front of it and built into your roof in some way. The following two photos illustrate two built-in batch heaters mounted high to allow gravity flow of the hot water.

This solar shower is just a 4" thick steel tank mounted high on the outdoor shower stall itself. We fill it up untill it overflows everyday and shower in the afternoon with a view of the mountains.

The photo on the opposite page illustrates a long thin batch heater at the base of the front face windows. It is built in below the solar glass and services a space on a lower level.

BATCH HEATER

Water is pumped into the tank from below until the tank overflows (outside or into a planter). The water is then heated by the sun and allowed to flow back down the same pipe that filled it and into the hot water lines. This involves some simple valving to close off the supply of cold water to fill the tank and open the hot water (gravity fed) to the hot water taps.

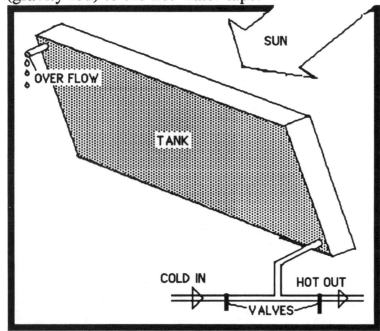

The valve arrangement shown can be located anywhere down in the dwelling. This tank is filled every morning and a few hours later (2 in the summer-4 in the winter) you have free hot water. Since the hot water is gravity fed to the taps the pressure is not very strong. This requires some custom easy flow fixtures or a mini booster pump.

The tank itself must be made of stainless steel. Regular steel tanks eventually rust out even when they are coated on the inside. If you want it to be permanent, use stainless steel. Any welder who can weld stainless steel can make the tank to your custom size with threaded fittings to receive pipes as shown in the diagram. After considering the factors of size discussed above the tank can be any size you want. The thickness should be 4" in the sunbelt areas. A thicker tank will hold more water but it will not get hot enough fast enough. A thinner tank will not hold enough water, will cool off faster and will get actually too hot. For areas with less sun outside the sun belt, go with a thinner tank (3") so it will heat up with less sun. This will make it hold less water so you may want to increase the surface area.

The tank must be insulated on three sides and glazed on the sun side with 1/4" thick tempered glass 1" from the surface of the tank. If the glass is not tempered, it will break from the heat. If it is closer to the tank than 1", it will break anyway. The sun side of the tank must be painted flat black. The stainless steel can be lightly sanded to give it a flat (not shiny) surface to hold the flat black paint. The temperatures are extreme so furnace, stove or engine paint must be used. Regular paint will peel.

This is the basic unit and how it works.

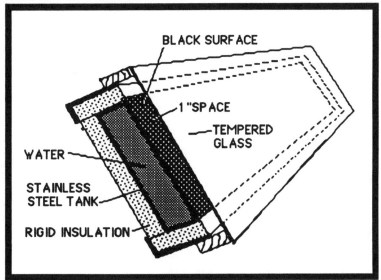

The unit should be installed with the glass face perpendicular to equinox (spring or autumn) sun. (see Earthship Vol. I, page 30) This will give you the best performance for the majority of the time. Ideally, for optimum performance the unit should be adjustable but the expense of doing this outweighs the added performance you get. Another option is to set the tank perpendicular to the winter solstice sun. This will give you the best winter performance. Summer performance will not be as good because the high sun will reflect off the glass. However, in the summer the water does not have to be as hot to be comfortable. In this case, reflectors as shown in the following diagram can increase summer performance.

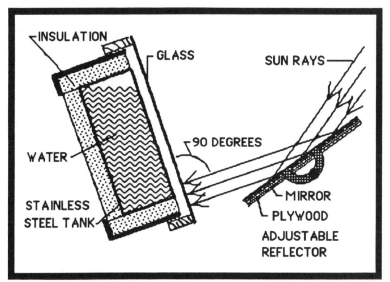

You want the reflectors (shiny metal or mirror on plywood) to be adjustable to reflect the sun so it hits the glass at a 90 degree or perpendicular angle. The sun reflects off of a surface at the same angle it comes in.

There are many different ways to detail a batch heater and there are even some (ugly) ready-made ones on the market. The best way to go is to have your own custom tailored solar batch heater built into your house.

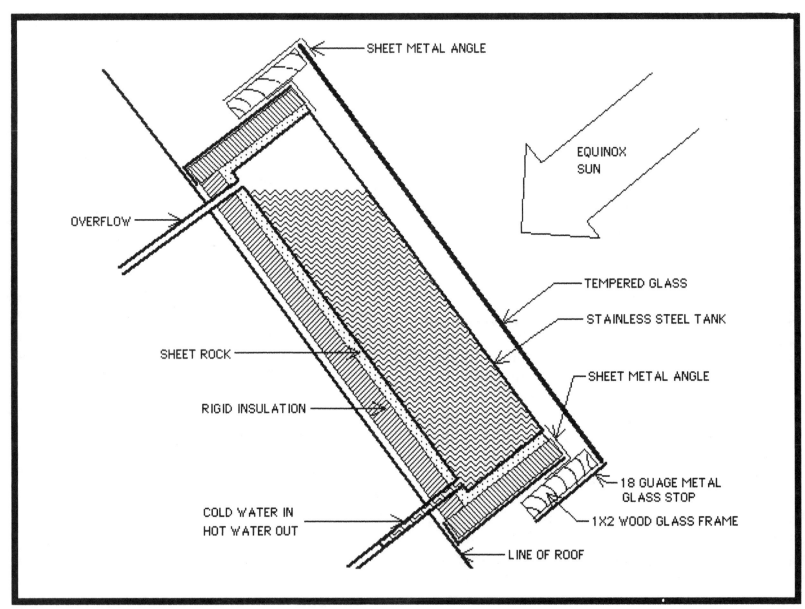

SHEET METAL ANGLE

EQUINOX
SUN

OVERFLOW

TEMPERED GLASS

STAINLESS STEEL TANK

SHEET ROCK

SHEET METAL ANGLE

RIGID INSULATION

18 GUAGE METAL
GLASS STOP

COLD WATER IN
HOT WATER OUT

1X2 WOOD GLASS FRAME

LINE OF ROOF

The above diagram shows actual construction detailing with a few more specifics than the previous schematics above.

Notice the layer of sheet rock between the tank and the insulation. This protects the insulation from melting when the tank gets hot. The sheetrock buffers the heat of the tank from all rigid insulation and from all wood. I have seen wood scorched by these tanks. Line the outside of the tank carefully and thoroughly with 1/2" sheetrock, making sure the stainless steel tank touches nothing but sheetrock. Also notice that the overflow is at the highest possible location on the tank. This is because it allows air to be displaced as water comes in. Without this your water pressure would blow the tank up like a balloon. Locate this overflow someplace very visible (preferably over a planter) so you can see when your tank is filled.

Ideal locations for batch heaters are high on the roof immediately above places where the hot water will be used. If the budget allows, it is ideal to have one over each bathroom. It is best to locate them in such a way (built into the roof) that the supply (water in and out) pipe never has to go outside. This will avoid any freezing problems in the pipe lines and keep detailing simple.

GAS *DEMAND* HOT WATER HEATERS

These heaters are wall mounted and take up very little space. They are roughly 18" wide, 13" deep, and 36" high. They must be located where they can be easily vented through the roof with a 6" double walled vent which takes a hole about 8" in diameter. They are usually mounted about three to four feet off of the floor. Cold water and the gas supply come in at the bottom and hot water goes out at the bottom.

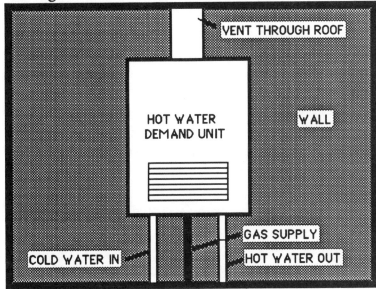

These units should be placed as near to the fixtures they will be servicing as possible. This will keep the time it takes to get hot water at the tap to a minimum. Remember, **the average sized demand unit allows you to use only one faucet at a time**, i.e. you can't take a shower while someone is washing dishes.

Due to their small size, demand units are easy to locate in the dwelling, however they must be allowed to get adequate combustion air. This means they can't be shut up in a tight closet. If they are in a small room or closet, the door must have louvers to let in air. Sometimes a dampered air vent (from the roof or through the wall) near the heater is necessary as some dwellings are so tight they don't allow enough combustion air for the flames. Most Earthships are vented so well in the summer *and* the winter that this is not necessary.

THE COMBO

The best of both worlds is the "combo" which is an ideal hot water system. It gives you free hot water from your batch heater when the sun allows. If you need hot water when there is no sun, you have your gas demand unit to provide it. The only drawback here is that you are essentially paying for two units. The total price here would be around $2500. The simplest way to set up this system is as two individual sources of hot water valved into the same line to the taps.

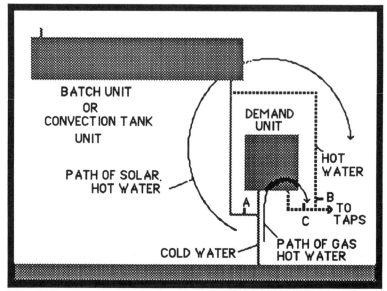

To fill the batch heater (every morning), open valve A and close B&C. When the tank is full close valve A. It remains closed during the use of both units, i.e. valve A is only opened to fill the batch tank. To use the batch heater, open valve B and close C. To use the demand heater, open valve C and close B. This gives you solar hot water whenever it is available and an unlimited supply of gas heated hot water when solar is not available. When no hot water is called for, a small pilot light burns. In homes with many bathrooms, you would want one of these systems for every two bathrooms or, if you can afford it, one for every bathroom. You can share one of these systems between kitchen and utility or kitchen and one seldom used bath.

This combo could also be used the same way with the convector tank unit instead of the batch heater for areas out of the sun-belt where a batch heater won't work. Hot water is very fun to use when you know it is free.

RECOMMENDATION

All things considered, our recommendation is to install a Paloma "on demand" gas hot water heater and to plumb for the addition of a batch heater or a convection heat storage unit. Install the batch heater or convection heat storage unit when you can afford it. This method will give you the most efficient, immediate and reliable fossil fueled hot water and provide you with the option of having free hot water when you can afford the luxury of the second system.

APPENDIX
Gas Demand Hot Water Heaters Made by Paloma
Order from SSA
Box 1041, Taos, NM 87571
(505) 758-9870
These units come in many sizes. The most common size is PH-16M-DP. This will work very well for one bath and a kitchen. There is a smaller size for an efficiency or studio structure and a larger size that will service two bathrooms. Be advised that the larger size uses more gas and

should not be used unless absolutely necessary. We recommend a smaller unit at each bathroom.

Gas Tank Hot Water Heaters Made by Nautilus
Order from SSA
Box 1041, Taos, NM 87571
(505) 758-9870
These units range in size from 40 to 114 gallons.

Convection Heat Storage Unit
These are not easy to obtain. A limited supply is available from SSA. These are units at a good price from a company that went out of business. Other companies are making them (more expensive) and we are in the process of obtaining a dealership. Order from SSA.
Box 1041, Taos, NM 87571
(505) 758-9870

Big Fin Made by ZomeWorks
Order from Zomeworks
1810 2nd Street, Santa Fe, NM
(505) 983-6929
This device requires a storage tank and pumps but can be mounted inside the solar face of the Earthship in the greenhouse, hallway heating duct. This allows it to work year round without freezing.

Copper Cricket Made by Sage Advance Corporation
Order from SSA
Box 1041, Taos, NM 87571
(505) 758-9870
This unit uses an existing gas hot water heater tank as a storage unit. It needs no pumps or electricity but installation in a new Earthship requires the use and and installation of a used hot water heater tank. Installed and working, it will cost you over $3000.

Filters Made by Mountain Filtration System
Order from SSA
Box 1041, Taos, NM 87571
(505) 758-9870
Send water sample to determine what type of filter you need to protect your gas demand hot water heater. This filter goes in right before the Paloma unit and may be in addition to your catch water filter described in Chapter 2.

5. LIGHTING
S Y S T E M S

"AND GOD SAID LET THERE BE LIGHT AND THERE WAS LIGHT." MAN SAID, LET THERE BE LIGHT AND THERE WERE NUCLEAR POWER PLANTS, UGLY POWER LINES, AND RADIOACTIVE WASTE.

LIGHTING HAS BECOME AN EXPENSIVE, *(ECOLOGICALLY AND ECONOMICALLY)* ENERGY CONSUMING ENDEAVOR IN CONVENTIONAL HOUSING. THE OBJECTIVES OF EARTHSHIP LIGHTING ARE TO SERIOUSLY REDUCE BOTH EXPENSE AND ENERGY REQUIREMENTS FOR PROVIDING DOMESTIC LIGHT. IN MANY CASES THE REDUCTION OF ENERGY USE HAS RESULTED IN AN INCREASE IN EXPENSE. THIS IS BECAUSE MANY OF THE NEW SOLAR ELECTRIC PRODUCTS DO NOT HAVE A LARGE ENOUGH MARKET TO BRING DOWN THE PRICES TO A COMPETITIVE AND REASONABLE LEVEL. ANOTHER FACTOR IS THAT THERE ARE SO MANY DIRECTIONS TO GO IN TERMS OF LIGHTING (AC VERSUS DC, INCANDESCENT VERSUS FLUORESCENT, ETC) AND EACH DIRECTION HAS ITS OWN CATALOG OF PRODUCTS THAT WORK FOR SPECIFIC SITUATIONS. THE BOTTOM LINE IS THAT, AT THIS POINT, NO STANDARD, SIMPLE, INEXPENSIVE DIRECTION FOR LIGHTING HAS BEEN ESTABLISHED FOR SOLAR DWELLERS. THE PURPOSE OF THIS CHAPTER, THEREFORE, WILL BE TO ESTABLISH THIS DIRECTION AND TO PRESENT THE CONCEPTS AND EQUIPMENT FOR SIMPLE, INEXPENSIVE "OFF THE POWER GRID" LIGHTING.

Fruit generally grows on trees. Animals and humans come along and pick it off and gather it or eat it on the spot. It is usually sized so that most creatures that harvest it can hold it in their hand or paw. Fruit is therefore accessible to all who want it through nature's <u>standardized method of production and delivery.</u>

Lighting (as well as construction detailing and all systems for conventional housing) has become standardized. It is through this standardization that various products have become both available and affordable to the general public. **This standardization is the one phenomenon of *existing* housing that we must align with in order to make new directions accessible to the masses.**

Having been involved in solar electric living for twenty years, both in terms of building for others and using it myself, I have observed some basic problems. These are not performance problems of the various products. They are problems related to the availability and standardization of the products as well as the initial design concepts themselves. Currently, solar housing presents the average homeowner with many directions and a multitude of varieties and types of bulbs and lights - few of which will work in existing fixtures without adaptations; all of which are more expensive than conventional fixtures and none of which are available at a local hardware store. Most of this equipment requires a technician for installation and sometimes a technician is even required for bulb replacement. This makes many new jobs for people who are hip to this equipment but it alienates the average homeowner who wants to be able to change a light bulb him/herself. The result here is that solar living is kept in a place where it is more difficult and expensive to use. Therefore, line grid electricity and the environmental price that goes along with it remains the immediately easiest and most accessible form of power to use for lighting for anyone other than environmental fanatics. This must change.

Conventional housing is loaded with inefficient fixtures that are readily available at the local Walmart or variety store. The replacement bulbs and repair parts for these fixtures are common and easy to understand for the typical handyman/homeowner and are also easy to find at your local variety store. **This availability and economic accessibility is a must for solar electricity to even begin to replace conventional electricity.**

The concepts and methods presented in this chapter may not be the ultimate in solar technology and do not come from the high tech specialized expertise of an electronics wizard.

They are aimed at making solar electricity available to the average person without requiring hours of study, thousands of dollars and/or a dependence on an expensive solar technician for maintenance of your lighting system.

CONCEPT
DAY TIME LIGHTING

The foremost aim of Earthship lighting is to get as much natural light from the sun as possible during daylight hours. This is an inherent feature of the Earthship design resulting from the admission of sun for heat and the use of skylights for ventilation. When locating skylights and solar glass, an awareness of domestic lighting needs in addition to heat and ventilation needs will be necessary. For example, a skylight that floods a light colored wall with reflected light is more effective than a skylight in the middle of a room. This is a good idea for work areas.

The skylight box itself can be painted a light color to maximize reflection of the in-coming rays.

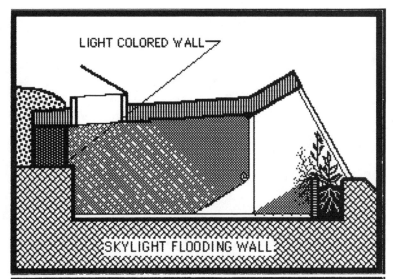

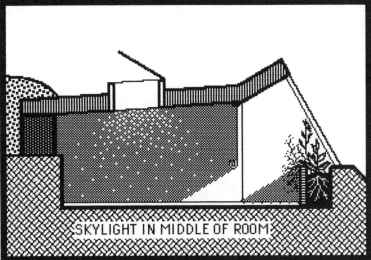

Skylights are needed for ventilation but should be kept to a minimum in cold climates. In temperate climates skylights can be used for almost all of the daytime lighting needs. See Chapter 8 for details of how to build operable skylights.

91

We recommend that you paint the back of each "U" a light color to reflect light but keep the walls dark out near the greenhouse where they can absorb the direct rays of the sun.

Lighting needs should be considered with regard to the front face glass when choosing shades for controlling the admission of heat. For example, shades that reduce sunlight coming through the front face can be <u>translucent</u> rather than <u>opaque</u>. This will reduce heat but allow light.

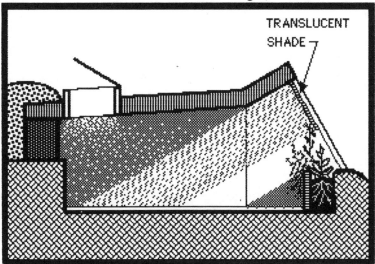

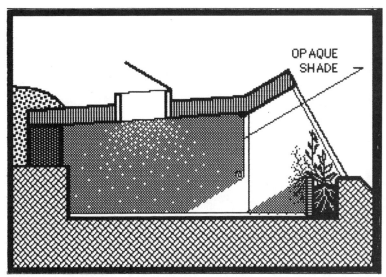

These techniques and the very nature of the Earthship design itself can almost eliminate the need for daytime lighting.

NIGHT LIGHTING

Night lighting can be broken into two categories, work lighting and atmosphere or general room lighting. This is a good method of delineating the AC and DC branches of the power system discussed on page 13 of Chapter 1. Work light is on AC power and room lighting is DC powered.

Work lighting

AC work lights are readily available in regular stores as are the replacement bulbs. They are plugged in to regular sockets, i.e. this is conventional equipment to start with. This is why all plug outlets are suggested to be on the AC branch of your system. The majority of work lights are conventional lamps bought in conventional stores that are part of the furnishings of a room as opposed to being built in. Therefore, other than the bulbs themselves which will be discussed later, work lighting is conventional AC equipment.

Room lighting

Room lighting is usually a broader usage of electricity involving more fixtures (sometimes indirect) and is generally used to light up the dwelling space overall. Room lighting does not necessarily involve moveable lamps as much as it does built-in fixtures to reflect and/or bounce light around the room creating an atmosphere or ambiance. Since this lighting usually involves more use of electricity than a particular spot light for working, it is suggested that the DC branch of your solar system be used directly for room lighting. It is not dependent on the inverter and will provide light without the 10% energy sacrifice of the inverted power <u>and</u> will provide light even if the inverter is down.

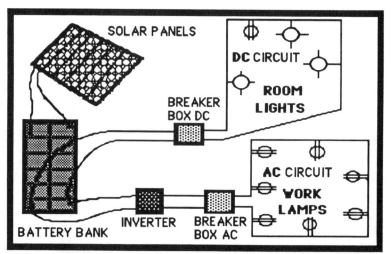

If the above concept is adopted, an occasional DC <u>plug</u> could still be added to the ROOM LIGHTING circuit to allow an occasional DC lamp. The "code required" AC plugs would still exist without interruption. The occasional DC plug on the room lighting circuit would simply be in addition to the DC room lighting.

EQUIPMENT

Both types of lighting discussed above obviously require bulbs. The conventional light bulbs bought in conventional stores are **incandescent** bulbs and are very inefficient. Most hardware stores either handle or can order both DC and AC incandescent light bulbs. Thus you can equip both your DC and your AC lighting with bulbs immediately or temporarily. **Fluorescent** bulbs use a fraction of the electricity that incandescent bulbs use. However, they have a reputation for providing white, unhealthy light and usually require special fixtures to accommodate the fluorescent tubes. They are usually known to be ugly and unhealthy but efficient. In recent years, **compact fluorescent** bulbs *that provide warm light and screw into regular lamp sockets* have become available in both DC and AC forms.

These bulbs (see appendix this chapter) make any conventional lamp or lighting fixture capable of being used in a solar system with no modifications. All you do is install an AC or a DC compact fluorescent bulb to almost any fixture and reduce your lighting electrical load by 60% to 80%.

The compact fluorescent bulbs require what is called a ballast to regulate the electricity to the bulb. This ballast is heavy and bulky and requires the shape and weight of the bulb to vary from that of a conventional light bulb. Both bulbs have what is called an Edison base (see following diagram). The Edison base is what allows them both to be screwed into a conventional lamp.

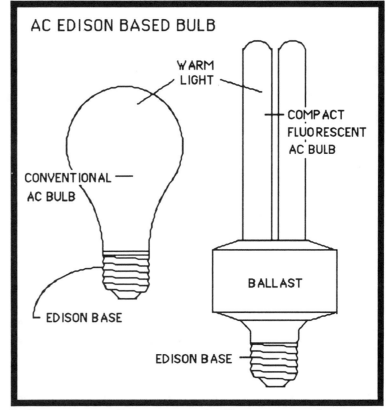

DC compact fluorescent bulbs are not in much demand. Consequently, they are not as refined in their design as the AC compact fluorescent bulb. They still can be obtained with Edison base which allows them to be used in a regular lamp.

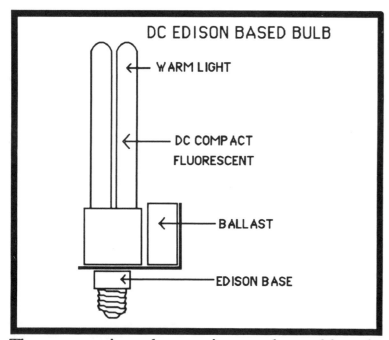

DC EDISON BASED BULB

WARM LIGHT

DC COMPACT
FLUORESCENT

BALLAST

EDISON BASE

There are various shapes, sizes, styles and brands of AC and DC compact fluorescents both for diffused and spot lighting much the same as conventional incandescent bulbs. The only ones worth considering are those with the ballast built in and an Edison base (screw into a regular socket as shown above). All others end up requiring more technical labor to install and maintain than they are worth.

One negative feature of the above DC compact fluorescent is that if your power system is not "hot" (strong voltage), the light takes a long time to come on. Sometimes, touching the bulb (thus grounding it) helps it light up faster. For this reason you should stay away from DC compact fluorescent fixtures with enclosed bulbs as they can't be touched.

The cost of compact fluorescent bulbs is considerably more than conventional incandescent bulbs but the life expectancy of the bulb is also considerably (up to 10 times) higher. The real issue is that they use a fraction of the electricity that common incandescent bulbs use thus allowing you to exist on a less expensive power system. (See appendix this chapter for obtaining compact fluorescent bulbs). Another objection to compact fluorescent bulbs is that some standardized lamp shades designed to clamp on the bulb itself will not work on the linear shape of the compact fluorescent.

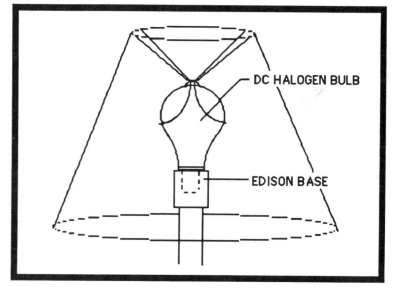

DC HALOGEN BULB

EDISON BASE

For these cases there is a DC halogen bulb that looks just like a regular light bulb. It is more efficient than DC incandescent bulbs but not as efficient as compact fluorescents. It is more expensive than DC incandescent bulbs but not as expensive as compact fluorescent. It is therefore the next best thing to compact fluorescent bulbs.

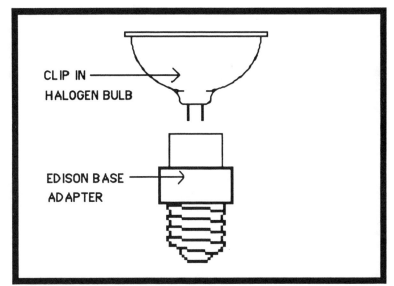

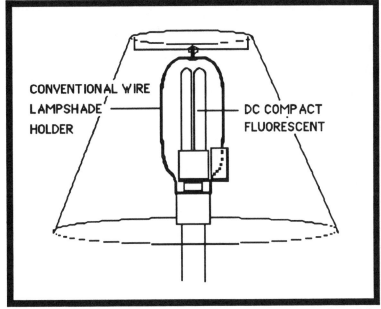

Both AC and DC compact flourescents work with conventional wire lamp shade holders.

There is also an Edison adaptor available for many types of clip-in halogen bulbs.

These adapt spot lights and many other types of lights to halogen use. Halogen lights however, are not as efficient as compact fluorescents. They are clearly a second choice on efficiency. Their selling point is that they provide more light with less wattage.

This is, however, often debatable. Soon there will be available an Edison based adaptor for a clip-in DC compact fluorescent bulb. This will increase the usage of these bulbs as the bulb often wears out before the ballast. This system is available now for AC compact fluorescent bulbs.

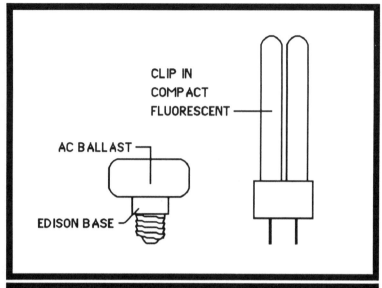

CLIP IN
COMPACT
FLUORESCENT

AC BALLAST

EDISON BASE

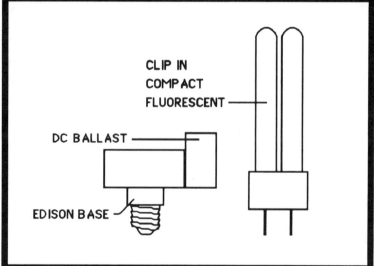

CLIP IN
COMPACT
FLUORESCENT

DC BALLAST

EDISON BASE

The information presented here is only a fraction of what is available. However, other types of efficient lighting are prohibitively expensive and difficult (at best) to service and maintain for the typical homeowner. People are accustomed to buying lamps and lighting fixtures wherever they want for a reasonable price and simply replacing the bulbs occasionally. The method of solar lighting discussed above allows this. Other methods do exist but they require so much money and frustration that they will not even be discussed in this chapter.

REVIEW OF BULBS

AC Incandescent - don't use except in emergency - available at local stores.

DC Incandescent - don't use except in emergency - available at local stores.

DC Halogen - can be used as a second choice - cheaper than compact fluorescent - available through SSA

DC Compact Fluorescent - <u>best DC choice -</u> less power than any other - most expensive - available through SSA

AC Compact Fluorescent - <u>best AC choice</u> - less power than any other - most expensive - available SSA

Halogen Clip-in, Edison based adapter - good for special situations - available through SSA

DC Compact Fluorescent, clip-in Edison base - good choice when available - available through SSA

AC Compact Fluorescent, clip-in Edison base - good choice when available - available through SSA

EXTERIOR LIGHTING

There are many exterior, self contained solar lights on the market. Few (if any) work for very long. It is better to use the same information presented in the first part of this chapter for exterior lighting. Simply use exterior lighting fixtures for the bulbs discussed previously.

There is one important fact to consider in Earthship exterior lighting. The exterior to the south can be lit up with interior lighting!

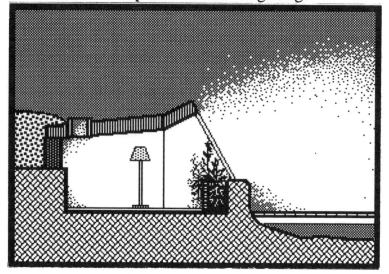

We recommend AC compact fluorescent, edison based bulbs for all AC lamps. They are reliable, provide warm light, last a long time, use a fraction of the power that anything else does and are easily available. AC clip-ins with Edison based adapters are a second choice as they are not as easy to obtain.

For DC lighting we suggest the DC compact fluorescent, edison based bulb with (awkward) built in ballast. Do not use it where you can't touch it. Again the DC clip-ins with Edison based adapters are a second choice as they are not as easy to obtain.

For places where the DC compact flourescent is inconvenient, use the edison based halogen DC bulb. It works just like a regular AC bulb and allows you to use any conventional fixture you want. Also the halogen adapter is a possibility there.

These recommendations cover the simple basic lighting needs for getting solar light in to the average home. More elaborate lighting will require a lighting consultant and greater expense, however, the basics presented in this chapter should still prevail whenever possible.

APPENDIX (DC in shaded area)

AC Compact Fluorescent Bulbs-with Edison base, 120 volts.

available wattages = equivalent AC incandescent

7w	40w
11w	60w
15w	75w
20w	100w
27w	120w

Last <u>10 times</u> longer than incandescent bulbs,
(Can not be used with a dimmer switch)

AC Clip-in Bulbs

AC Compact Fluorescent Adapters - available in wattages similar to AC compact fluorescent bulbs

DC Compact Flourescent Bulbs-with Edison base, 12 volt

available in wattages equivalent to:

= 25w AC incandescent
= 40w   "   "
= 50w   "   "
= 60w   "   "   (Can not be used with a dimmer switch)

DC Clip-in Bulbs

DC Compact Fluorescent Adapters - available in wattages, similar to DC compact fluorescent bulbs

Halogen Edison Based Bulbs - 12 volt

available wattages = equivalent AC incandescent watts

21w	50w
35w	75w
50w	100w

Halogen Adapters - 12volt, with clip-in bulbs available in 50 watt.

Order from: Solar Survival Architecture, P.O. Box 1041, Taos, New Mexico, 87571 505 758- 9870

A PARABLE ABOUT LIGHT

ONCE THERE WERE MANY PEOPLE TRAPPED IN A DARK
CAVERN. THEY STUMBLED AROUND IN THE DARKNESS AFRAID
AND SUFFERING. GOD LOOKED DOWN UPON THESE PEOPLE
AND DECIDED TO HELP THEM. A BEAUTIFUL BEAM OF LIGHT
WAS SENT DOWN TO SHINE UPON A **DOOR** THAT OPENED INTO
A PASSAGEWAY WHICH WOULD TAKE THEM OUT OF THE
DARKNESS FOREVER.
THE PEOPLE SAW THIS BEAM OF LIGHT.
THEY BECAME VERY JOYOUS AND BEGAN TO WORSHIP THE
LIGHT.
THEY PERFORMED RITUALS AND MEDITATED ON THE LIGHT.
THEY DANCED AND SANG IN THE LIGHT.
THEY TRIED TO PULL OTHERS INTO THE LIGHT.
THEY ERECTED MONUMENTS TO THE LIGHT.
THEY DRESSED IN WHITE CLOTHING TO LOOK LIKE THE LIGHT.
THEY MADE PICTURES AND SYMBOLS OF THE LIGHT.
THEY GAZED AT AND PRAYED TO THE LIGHT.
THEY WROTE SONGS AND STORIES ABOUT THE LIGHT.
THIS WAS VERY BEAUTIFUL, BUT THEY NEVER SAW
THE **DOOR**.

PART TWO
COMPONENTS OF THE EARTHSHIP

6. ADOBE FIREPLACES
C O M P O N E N T S

MOST HOUSES ARE KEPT TOO WARM (AT THE EXPENSE OF THE OWNER AND THE ENVIRONMENT) BY THEIR VARIOUS HEATING SYSTEMS. IT IS MUCH MORE HEALTHY TO KEEP AN INTERIOR ENVIRONMENT JUST A BIT ON THE COOL SIDE. ONE REASON FOR THIS IS THAT WHEN THE *DIFFERENCE* IN TEMPERATURE BETWEEN INDOORS AND OUTDOORS IS NOT SO RADICAL, THE HUMAN BODY HAS LESS ADJUSTING TO DO WHEN GOING FROM INSIDE TO OUTSIDE. THIS REDUCES STRESS ON THE HUMAN BODY THUS MAKING IT STRONGER TO RESIST ILLNESS OR DISEASE. THE EXISTING ACCEPTED COMFORT ZONE IS BETWEEN 70 AND 80 DEGREES FARENHEIT. IT SHOULD BE BETWEEN 60 AND 70 DEGREES F. THIS WOULD BE HEALTHIER FOR THE HUMAN BODY AND EASIER TO ACHIEVE WITH A THERMAL MASS HOME AS THE TEMPERATURE OF THE EARTH ITSELF (BELOW THE SURFACE) IS CLOSE TO 60 DEGREES. EARTHSHIPS CAN BE DESIGNED, DETAILED AND OPERATED SUCH THAT THEY CAN HOLD A STABLE TEMPERATURE WITHIN THE 60-70 DEGREE COMFORT ZONE. SERIOUS HEATING *SYSTEMS* ARE NOT NEEDED. IN MOST CASES, A SIMPLE AND BEAUTIFUL FIREPLACE IS ENOUGH IN THE WINTER TO TEMPER THE ENVIRONMENT INSIDE AN EARTHSHIP TO A LEVEL OF COMFORT ACCEPTABLE TO MOST HUMANS. THIS CHAPTER WILL EXPLAIN THE PRINCIPLES AND METHODS OF BUILDING AN ADOBE FIREPLACE.

Since a fireplace is simply needed for mild tempering of the environment in an Earthship, it need not be a serious, super efficient fireplace. It will not be used enough for heat to warrant the expense of a high tech, super fireplace. Fireplaces in Earthships are used mainly for atmosphere and light duty heat tempering. A simple adobe fireplace that draws well, and doesn't smoke is all most Earthships need. Adobe fireplaces can cost as much as you want to spend, as they have become an art form which is always license to charge a fortune. The truth is that there is about $150 maximum in materials in an adobe fireplace, and the equivalent of about four full days of labor for one person. (This doesn't include plastering, which is part of the wall finishing process.)

Adobe fireplaces need not be limited to the Southwest. They are obviously easier to build there, due to the fact that adobes can easily be bought in the Southwest. It takes about 100 adobe bricks to build an adobe fireplace. One hundred adobes is a full pallet. This would cost about $60.00 plus freight. It would be as easy to ship one hundred adobes anywhere in the country as it would to ship regular bricks. However, shipping of materials is never as good as using something made locally. Adobes can be made anywhere there is enough sun to dry them. Making 100 adobes would not be very difficult. There are

many books already written about making adobes. If you want to make your own adobes, check the appendix of this chapter for "how to" books on adobe making. See this appendix also for where to purchase adobes. You want 4"x8"x12" adobes.

SIZING THE FIREPLACE

There is a required relationship between the stack or flue size of a fireplace and the mouth size. The area of the flue must not be smaller than 1/8 the area of the mouth.

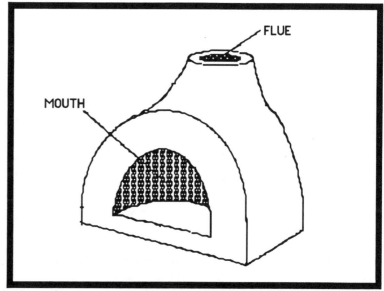

This formula must be followed to keep the fireplace from smoking. A good size for an average adobe fireplace is a 12" diameter flue and a 26" by 26" mouth.

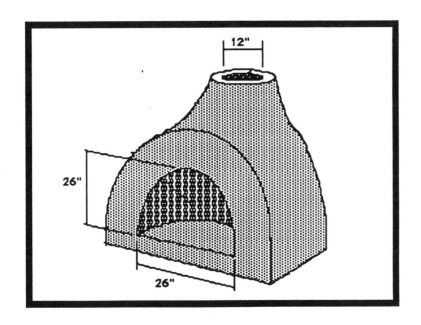

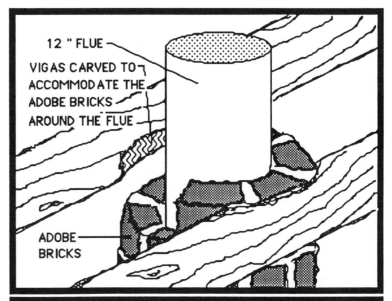

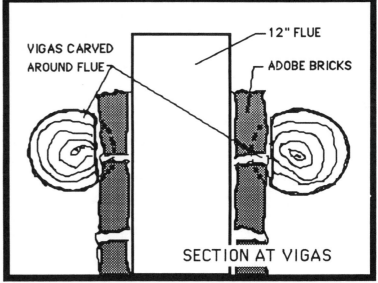

LOCATING THE FIREPLACE

The fireplace must be located so the flue will pass between two roof beams with six inches of adobe brick between the metal flue and the wood beams. The flue can be 12" diameter galvanized furnace pipe. It need not last forever as it is simply a form and/or liner for the adobe brick flue.

A wood box out of 2x12 stock is usually made to accommodate the fireplace flue. This is very similar to the skylight boxes detailed on page 114 of Earthship Volume I. This box is installed as the roof decking goes on. This allows the roof insulation and roofing to be totally detailed out and weather-proofed before the fireplace is built.

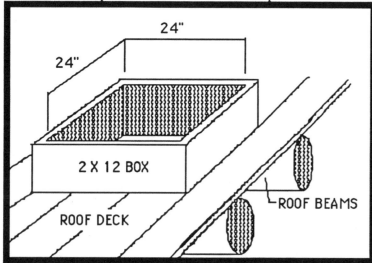

The interior dimension of this box should be 24" x 24". This allows a 12" diameter flue with 6" of adobe all around it to pass through. The beams in this particular space must either be placed far enough apart to accommodate this 24" clearance or they can be carved slightly to allow it.

Once this roof box is installed over the approximate location of the fireplace you are ready to precisely locate the fireplace. Find the center of the skylight box by laying two sticks across the top, corner to corner. Drop a plumb bob down from the intersection of the two sticks.

This locates the center of the flue of the fireplace.

The center of the flue of the fireplace is about 12"
from the front face of the fireplace so this also
locates the front of the fireplace.

BUILDING THE FIREPLACE
FOUNDATION
The fireplace should set on an 8" thick concrete
foundation. This foundation is usually about 4'-
6"x 4'-6" for an average sized fireplace against a
wall. This will accommodate the fireplace and
the hearth. The hearth is a code required
extension in front of the fireplace usually about
16" thick.

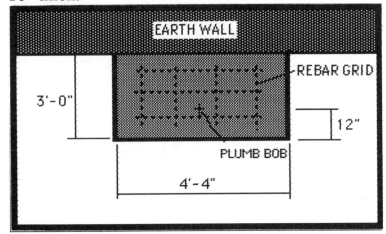

WALL FIREPLACE

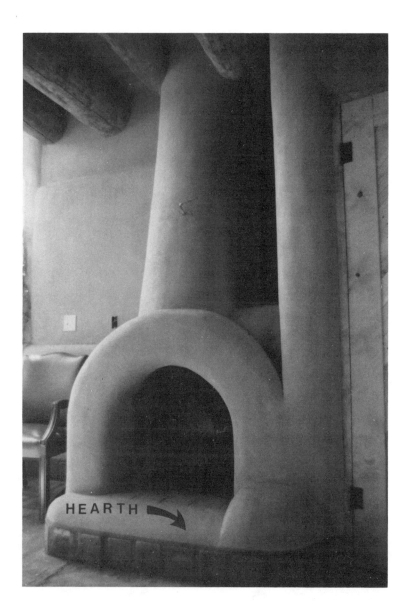

Corner fireplaces would also require a 4'-6" wide foundation, however, they are shaped a little differently, going all the way back into the corner. In both cases, center the foundation with the plumb bob from the center of the roof box.

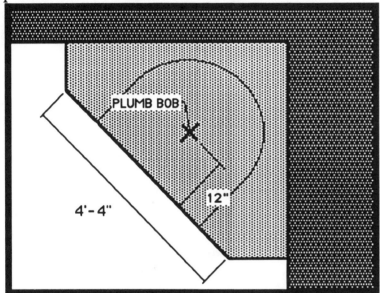

CORNER FIREPLACE FOUNDATION

It is a good idea to lay out your fireplace on the dirt before you pour your foundation. This will insure the proper foundation size. The mix for the foundation should be a 3-4-5 mix. That is: 3 parts portland cement, four parts sand and five parts gravel added to water. The mix should be barely loose enough to pour. The foundation should have a 12" grid (see diagram previous page) of half inch rebar placed in the middle of the pour (4" from the bottom). The top of this

foundation should be at the level of your subfloor. Therefore, it can usually be formed by simply digging the appropriate sized 8" deep shape out of the earthen subfloor.

Once the foundation is poured, you can immediately lay the adobe base for the fireplace. This is done by laying adobes (which are 4" thick) up to the height that you want the fireplace above the finished floor. This height is usually about eight inches and involves at least two layers of adobes. Stagger the joints of the adobes so that no second layer joint is directly over a first layer joint. All that is necessary now is the base for the fireplace. The hearth comes later. The base begins 12" out from the plumbob which marks the center of your flue.

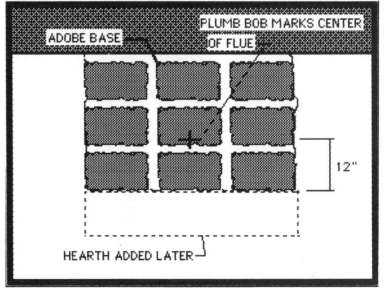

Adobes can be cut with a hand axe. Score the adobe deeply all the way around where you want to cut it and then hack it right on the score mark. You will break a few trying to learn this.

THE MOUTH

The next step is to make a form for the mouth of the fireplace. This is made from any rigid foam insulation. It should be 4" thick to support the adobes. Typical size is 28" high and 28" wide. The mud plaster will eventually bring both these dimensions down to the recommended 26" high by 26" wide.

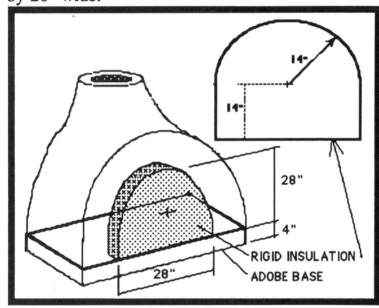

Place this form on the front edge of your adobe base. Now you can begin laying the 4"x8"x12" adobes around the form to make the box.

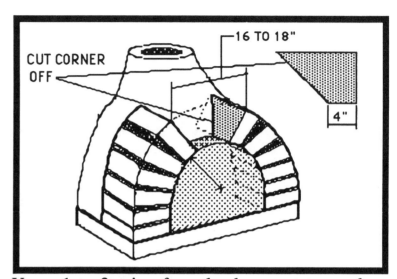

Use a 1 to 3 mix of portland cement to sand to bond the bricks together. This mix should be quite stiff (not runny). The first few bricks on either side will be stacked right on top of each other and laid with the 8" dimension facing out. When you get into the arch notice that all bricks are aimed at the center of the rigid foam form. Mark this center point clearly so it will be easy to aim at. Lay the bricks all the way up until there is a space at the very top of 16" to 18" between the top corners of the top bricks. This is the space for the "key brick". Notice that the bottom corner of the two top bricks is cut off. It is cut off as shown in the inset diagram above. Now you are ready to place the key brick. The key brick is laid standing up on its 4" edge. The corners are cut off to conform to the space left for it.

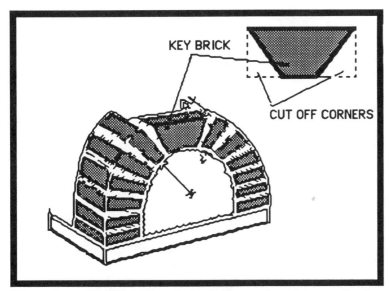

KEY BRICK

CUT OFF CORNERS

The above process of building the face of the fireplace can be done in two work sessions. Go halfway up the first session and let the cement set up a day. Then go all the way to the key brick.

THE OVEN

The oven can be built while the face is being built. It also takes two or three sessions to build. It starts by standing the bricks on end (in mortar) around a chalk line drawn on the foundation 28" deep and 28" wide.

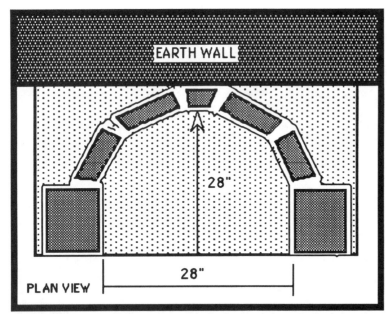

Notice the bricks are slightly wedged (with the hand axe) to fit together better.

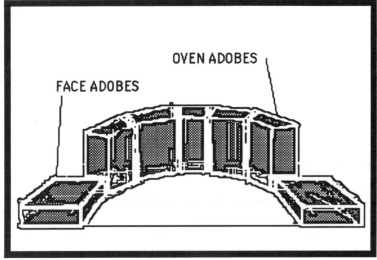

Now another course of oven adobes standing up

on edge is laid on top of the first course. This happens as the face is going up. **Don't let any joints in the second course occur over joints in the first course.**

The second course must also lean slightly toward the center to begin the funnel effect to the 12" diameter flue. The next few courses are done with half bricks. This allows a sharper arc at the top of the oven as the space gets smaller and constricts toward the flue. Keep leaning toward the 12" diam. flue opening and don't let any joints occur over joints below. This makes a stronger overall unit.

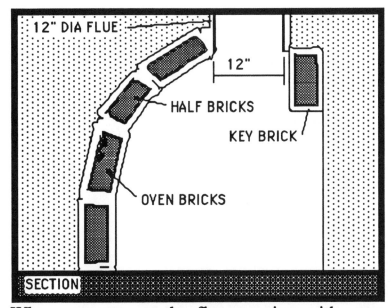

When you get to the flue opening with your adobe work, you will be ready to place the 12" diameter galvanized flue liner. Simply set it in position (as shown in the diagram above). Slightly insert it into the opening and pack cement around it. It is a 2'-0" or 3'-0" length of galvanized furnace pipe. This first section of your flue liner is where the damper usually goes.

DAMPER

The purpose of a damper in this kind of fireplace is to block the flue when the fireplace is not in use so that back drafts from wind will not blow into your room and spread ashes all around. It is also used to block cold winter air from dropping down into the room when the fireplace is not in

use. As a rule, dampers are kept open only when the fireplace is in use and closed the rest of the time. Occasionally, they are opened in the summer to aid in ventilation. The fireplace must be clean of all ashes during this time to prevent ashes from blowing back into the room.

The damper is made from a disk of 16 gauge sheet metal screwed to a 1/2" square steel rod. The disk is just large enough in diameter to scrape the sides of the galvanized metal flue liner when closed. This friction fit is all that is needed to keep the damper closed.

The steel rod must be long enough to penetrate one side of the flue liner and extend about one inch. It must also extend through the adobe chimney on the other side and bend down for a handle in the room . This usually takes about 20" overall plus another four inches to bend down for a handle.

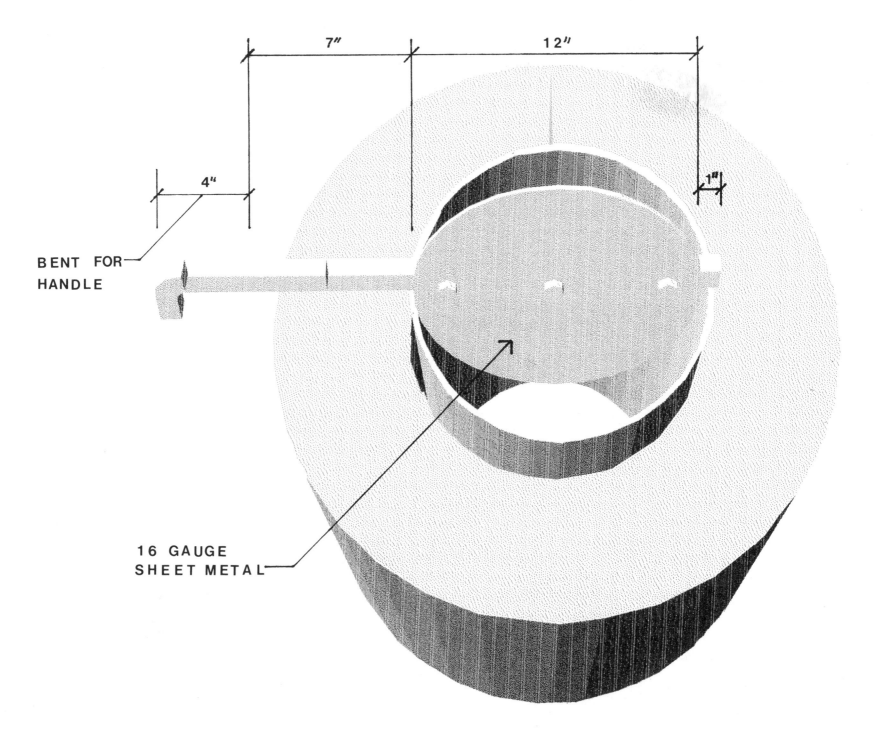

7"

12"

4"

1"

BENT FOR
HANDLE

16 GAUGE
SHEET METAL

116

The damper can be ordered from a sheet metal shop. The steel rod is drilled to receive at least three small bolts for holding the disk to the rod. Upon installation, the disk is unscrewed and the rod is inserted through two holes punched into the galvanized flue liner. The holes must be aligned at the same height and 180 degrees apart.

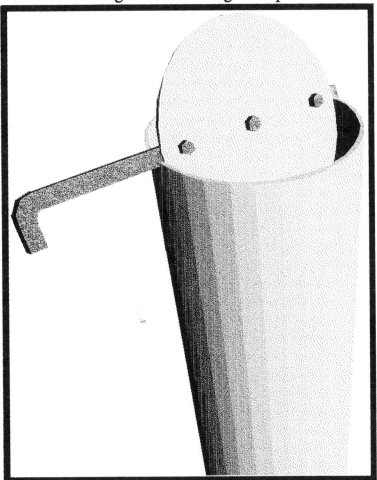

Insert the rod and then bolt the 16 ga. steel disk back on. Now the bolts must be bent on the ends to prevent the disk from coming loose. It would be very difficult if not impossible to re-install it after the fireplace is finished.

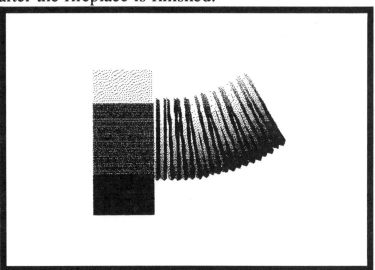

With the first section of flue liner and damper installed, you are ready to begin the chimney. Half adobe bricks are used for the chimney. They are laid around the flue liner in cement with staggered coursing (no joints over other joints below). You can only go about two courses at a time. Then you must stop to let the cement set up before you do two more. Every course should have two double strands of bailing wire wrapped around it as a banding strap.

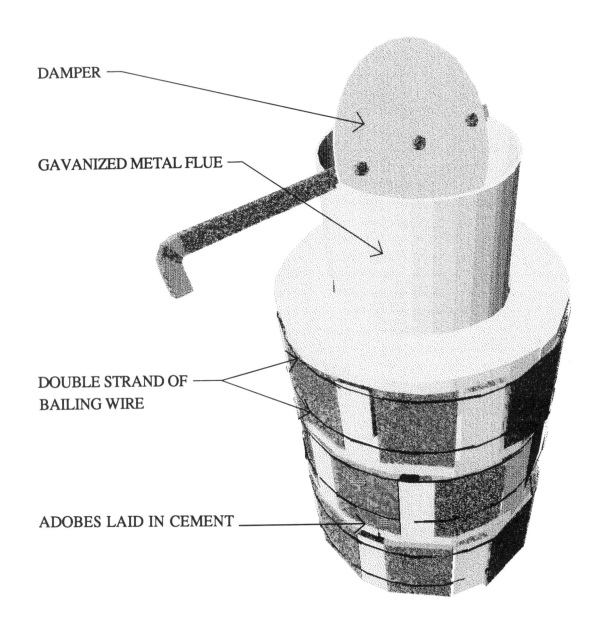

DAMPER

GAVANIZED METAL FLUE

DOUBLE STRAND OF
BAILING WIRE

ADOBES LAID IN CEMENT

The chimney is now taken up to the roof box described on page 108. At the bottom of the roof box the adobe stops.

FLUE LINER 2'
ABOVE ROOF

The flue liner is extended up at least two feet above the roof. It must be two feet above anything within ten feet from it.

COMBUSTION AIR DUCT

Earthships have the potential of being shut up very tight with few, if any, drafts. For this reason a 4" diameter fresh combustion air duct must be installed at the base of the mouth of the fireplace. It is best made from a flexible metal duct material (see Appendix, Chapter 6). It is laid in place and built into part of the hearth, tucked into a corner then taken out through a corner of the wood roof box.

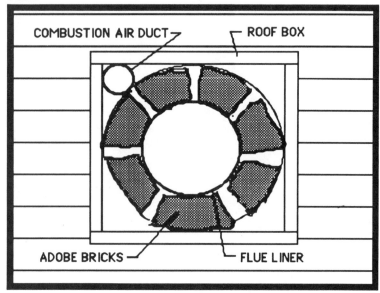

COMBUSTION AIR DUCT — ROOF BOX

ADOBE BRICKS — FLUE LINER

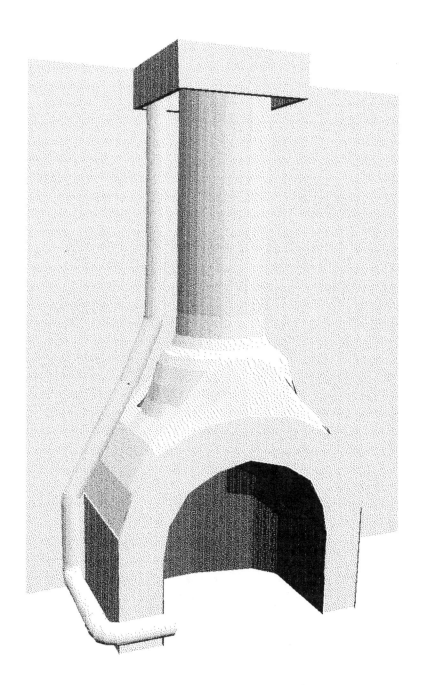

121

Outside and above the roof, the cumbustion air duct is turned out and down and poured into a pumicecrete (light weight concrete) chimney cowling.

A form made from metal lath is built around the metal flue liner for a height of at least 12" above the roof box. This is to form the poured pumicecrete exterior portion of the chimney.

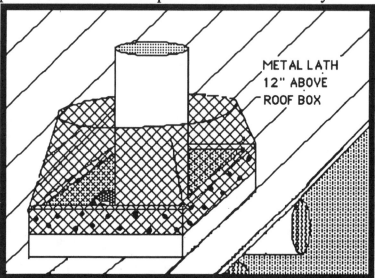

Adobe will deteriorate when used on the exterior. For this reason the pumicecrete (made from three parts cement to ten parts pumice) is used. If pumice is hard to find, regular sand/cement (3 to 1) can be used, however, pumice is lighter and is a better material for this application. Silicone caulking is now applied around the joint between the pumicecrete and the flue liner and then conventional scratch plaster and stucco are used to finish the short chimney extension.

A wind/rain hood is used to help prevent back drafts and rainfall down the chimney. They can be ordered from your local sheet metal shop. Twelve inch rain hoods are sometimes hard to find. If this is the case you can have your local sheet metal shop make one as per the accompanying diagram.

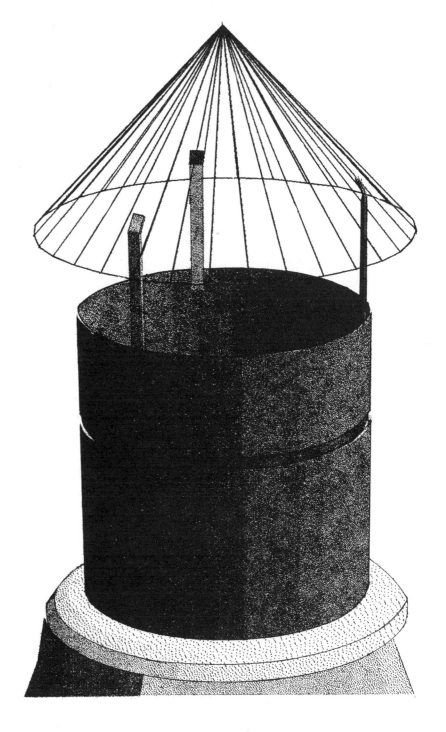

You now have a functional fireplace. It can be finished as per the mud plaster instructions in Chapter 9, Volume I. Where wood or carpet floors are used, a 16" minimum hearth is recommended. A custom screen can be made by shaping 3/8" rebar to the mouth of the fireplace and wiring 1/4" hardware cloth to the rebar frame.

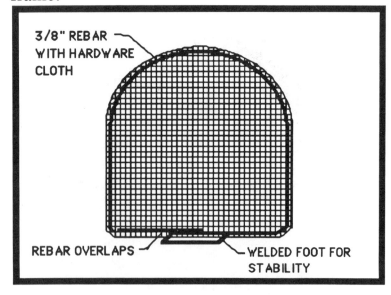

3/8" REBAR
WITH HARDWARE
CLOTH

REBAR OVERLAPS

WELDED FOOT FOR
STABILITY

Following are some typical Earthship fireplaces.

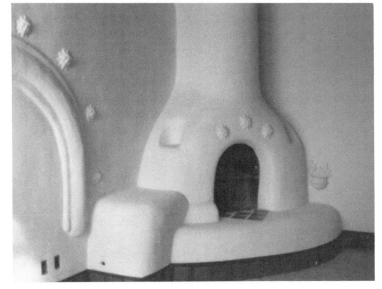

APPENDIX

Flexiliner
4" flexible flue liner comes in a variety of extendable lengths.
Order from SSA
Box 1041, Taos, NM 87571
(505) 758-9870

Adobes
Order from Adobe Factory
PO Box 165
Alcalde, NM 87511
(505) 852-4131

Books on Making Adobes
Adobe Bricks in New Mexico by Edward Smith
Published by New Mexico Bureau of Mines and Mineral Resources

Adobe and Rammed Earth Buildings - Design and Construction by Paul Graham McHenry, Jr.
University of Arizona Press

Adobe: A Comprehensive Bibliography by Rex C. Hopson
The Lightning Tree - Jene Lyon Publishing

These books available at Moby Dickens Bookshop 124-A Bent St. Taos, NM 87571 (505) 758-3050, or check with your local public library.

7. STAIRWAYS
C O M P O N E N T S

A STAIRWAY CAN SIMPLY BE A WAY OF GETTING FROM ONE FLOOR TO THE NEXT OR IT CAN BE A PIECE OF SCULPTURE THAT ADDS BEAUTY AND GRACE TO THE HOME WHILE PROVIDING TRAVEL BETWEEN LEVELS. CONVENTIONAL STAIRWAYS ARE USUALLY COMPLICATED AND EXPENSIVE IF THEY HAVE THIS BEAUTY AND GRACE. IF THEY ARE FAIRLY SIMPLE AND INEXPENSIVE, THEY USUALLY ADD NOTHING TO THE HOME AND SOMETIMES DETRACT FROM IT. THE METHOD OF BUILDING STAIRWAYS PRESENTED IN THIS CHAPTER ALLOWS FOR AN INEXPENSIVE STAIRWAY THAT CAN BE BEAUTIFUL, GRACEFUL *AND* SIMPLE - SIMPLE ENOUGH THAT AN UNSKILLED HOMEOWNER CAN DESIGN AND BUILD ONE HIM/HERSELF.

A CONVENTIONAL STAIRWAY IN A FRAME HOUSE IS MADE WITH THE SAME MATERIALS AND SKILLS THAT THE HOUSE ITSELF IS MADE OF, THOUGH THE TECHNIQUES ARE SOMEWHAT MORE DIFFICULT. AN EARTHSHIP STAIRWAY ALSO EMPLOYS THE SAME MATERIALS AND SKILLS USED IN BUILDING THE INITIAL BUILDING, HOWEVER, IN THIS CASE, THE TECHNIQUES ARE NO MORE DIFFICULT THAN THOSE USED IN BUILDING THE HOME. ONE INITIAL PURPOSE OF THE EARTHSHIP DESIGN WAS TO MAKE IT AVAILABLE TO AND WITHIN THE GRASP OF THE AVERAGE PERSON. THE SAME IS TRUE WITH THE COMPONENTS OF THE EARTHSHIP. *IF YOU CAN BUILD AN EARTHSHIP, YOU CAN BUILD AN EARTHSHIP STAIRWAY.*

THE BASICS OF A STAIRWAY

The first step in building a stairway is sizing. This is accomplished by determining the rise and the run of the stairway. The rise is the total distance you want to travel (vertically) between levels, i.e. the floor to floor distance. The run is how far (horizontally) it will take you to travel the vertical distance.

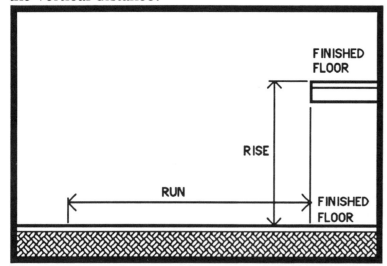

The rise is made up with a series of **risers** all of which should be about 8" tall. The run is made up of a series of **treads** all of which should be about 12" wide. These sizes make a comfortable stair for the average sized human.

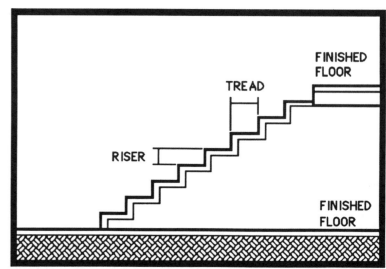

Now, to size your stairway you take your floor to floor height and convert it to inches and divide by eight. This will tell you how many risers you need to go the distance. If it doesn't come out even with 8" then some fraction close to (over or under) 8" will do.

EXAMPLE - Floor to floor distance is 10'-0". This is 120 inches. 120 divided by 8 is 15. Therefore you would have 15 risers.

You always have one less tread than risers because the upper level itself is the last tread. Therefore, the stair in the above example would have 14 treads. Since each tread wants to be about 12", the total run on this stair would be 14'-0".

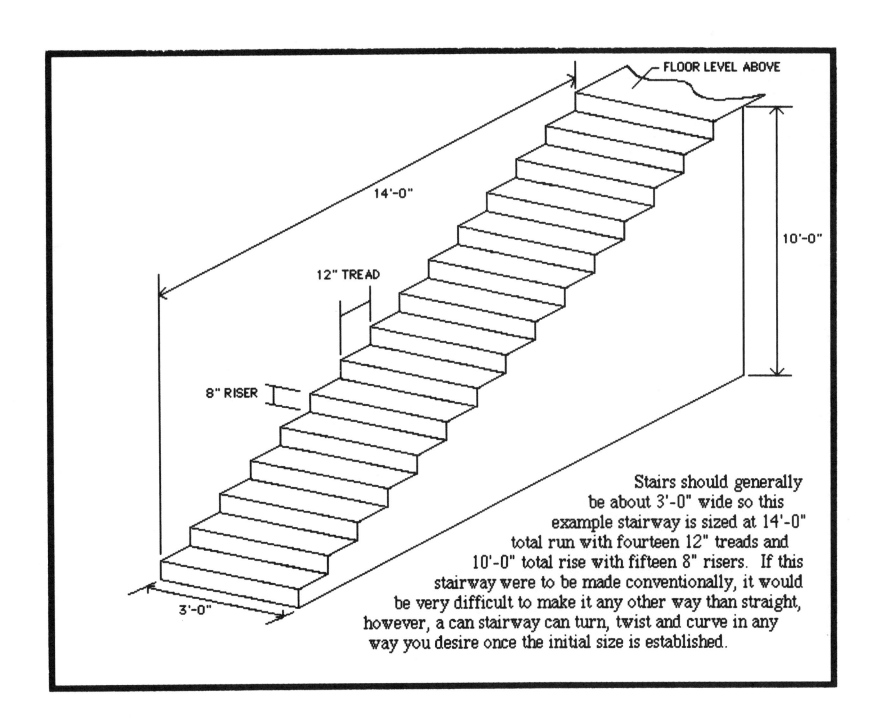

FLOOR LEVEL ABOVE

14'-0"

10'-0"

12" TREAD

8" RISER

3'-0"

Stairs should generally be about 3'-0" wide so this example stairway is sized at 14'-0" total run with fourteen 12" treads and 10'-0" total rise with fifteen 8" risers. If this stairway were to be made conventionally, it would be very difficult to make it any other way than straight, however, a can stairway can turn, twist and curve in any way you desire once the initial size is established.

132

CONSTRUCTION

Once you know the size of your stairway you simply draw it on the floor and wall (if it is against a wall) and begin building. The treads are made from wood 2x12's or 3x12's that span between two can walls. The can walls go up to the height of the first tread then it is installed. The treads are laid into the same cement mortar that the cans are laid in.

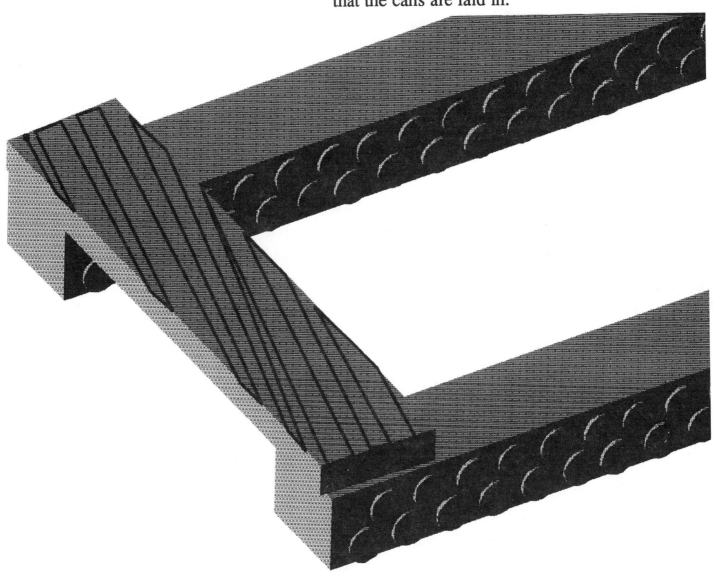

16d nails are nailed halfway into the underside ends of the wood treads to cleat the tread to the cement.

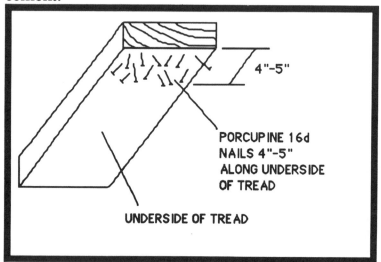

PORCUPINE 16d NAILS 4"-5" ALONG UNDERSIDE OF TREAD

4"-5"

UNDERSIDE OF TREAD

The tread is then pushed into a fat patty of cement on the can wall and leveled both ways with a torpedo level (a short level).

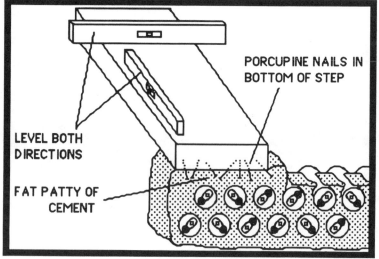

PORCUPINE NAILS IN BOTTOM OF STEP

LEVEL BOTH DIRECTIONS

FAT PATTY OF CEMENT

When the cement dries, the tread is firmly fastened to the cement of the can wall. This is essentially the same as nailing the tread to the cement/can wall. This technique is called porcupining - the treads are porcupined then laid into the cement. Next the can walls go up to the height of the second tread then it is installed with the *porcupine technique* previously described.

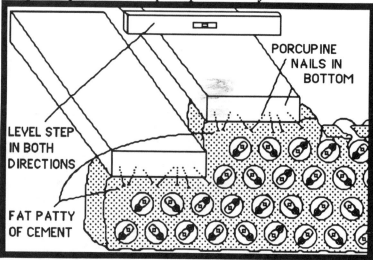

PORCUPINE NAILS IN BOTTOM

LEVEL STEP IN BOTH DIRECTIONS

FAT PATTY OF CEMENT

Then the can walls go up to the height of the third tread and it is installed, etc. Can laying is discussed on page 158 of Earthship Vol. I and in Chapter 9 of this volume. The treads (via the porcupine detail) become an integral part of the structure. When laying the porcupined tread on the can wall ledger, be sure to allow a "fat patty" of cement to receive the porcupined nails coming out of the tread.

There are two different purposes for the can walls. One is to make a <u>ledger</u> for the treads to set on and the other is to make the <u>railing</u>. This can be achieved in two ways.

<u>The ledger wall can also be the railing.</u> In this case porcupine the top of the tread with 1-1/2" roofing nails. The ledger wall is then taken over the top of the tread to become the railing. The bottom of the tread is porcupined with 16d nails.

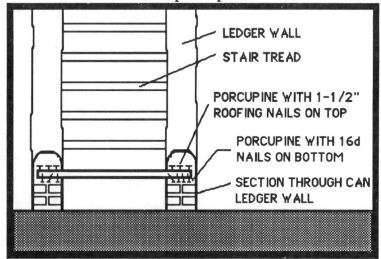

LEDGER WALL

STAIR TREAD

PORCUPINE WITH 1-1/2" ROOFING NAILS ON TOP

PORCUPINE WITH 16d NAILS ON BOTTOM

SECTION THROUGH CAN LEDGER WALL

<u>The railing wall can be in addition to the ledger wall.</u> This just makes for a stronger more durable stairway and is advised where ever possible. When this method is used, both the railing and the ledger wall should go up at the same time to the height of the treads as this bonds them together better.

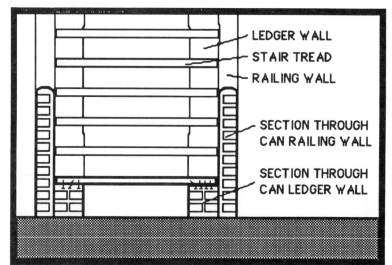

LEDGER WALL

STAIR TREAD

RAILING WALL

SECTION THROUGH CAN RAILING WALL

SECTION THROUGH CAN LEDGER WALL

If the stair is against a wall, a ledger wall for the treads is all that is needed on the wall side.

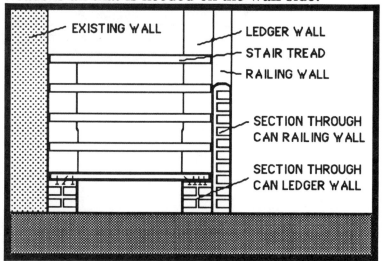

EXISTING WALL

LEDGER WALL

STAIR TREAD

RAILING WALL

SECTION THROUGH CAN RAILING WALL

SECTION THROUGH CAN LEDGER WALL

136

When all the treads have been installed, the stairway is structurally finished. The risers are now added. The treads are laid with the front of the upper tread in plane (lined up) with the back of the lower tread.

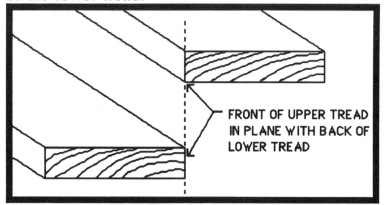

Install a wood shim 3/4" thick (as shown below) to the back of the lower tread with screws.

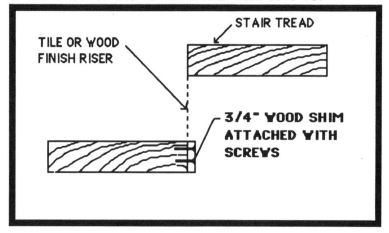

The riser backing can now be installed to this shim again with screws. This piece is 3/4" plywood and is also screwed (at an angle) into the upper tread.

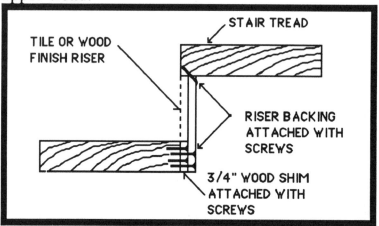

The first and lowest riser is too close to the floor to allow the above method. Bottom risers are usually built with can and mortar fill. This method may also be used for the second tread for the same reason.

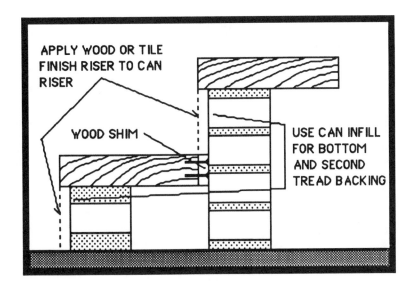

Now a tile finish or a wood finish riser can be installed. If a wood finish riser is used, the bottom riser can be glued (with liquid nails) to the smoothly plastered bottom can riser. The plaster must be allowed to cure for one week before a wood riser is glued to it. The following photo illustrates tile risers.

If a recessed riser is desired, the 3/4" shim can be increased to 1 1/2".

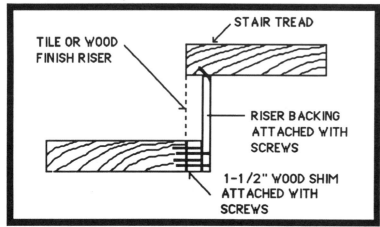

Another method of achieving a recess is to let the treads overlap each other by 1/2" to 3/4".

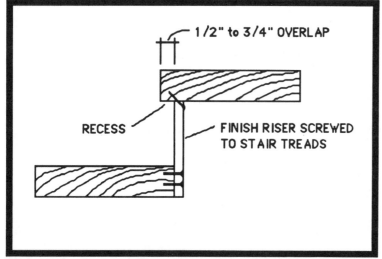

The entire can wall stairway can now be plastered using the techniques described in Chapter 9 of Earthship Vol. I. Due to the nature of can walls,

any shape or curve or twist can be built in to the stairway. The shape is drawn on the floor and the can walls follow the drawing. Be sure to allow for the finished floor when laying out the first tread.

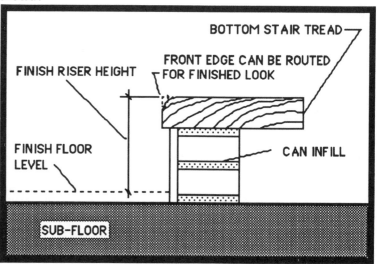

Routing the front edge of the tread with a 1/2" round bit gives it a smooth, finished look.

These stairways can be carpeted or finished with tile, flagstone or other floor materials. The heights of the treads would have to be lowered by whatever thickness the finish materials require.

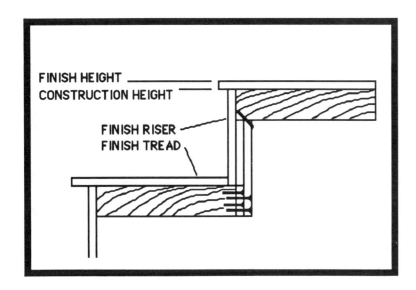

FINISH HEIGHT
CONSTRUCTION HEIGHT

FINISH RISER
FINISH TREAD

It is easiest and most economical, however, to allow the 3x12 construction tread to simply be the finish tread.

Do not try to lay more than three treads per day and lay these in three different sessions spaced about 1-1/2 hours apart to allow the cement to partially cure on one tread before attempting another. Cement takes seven days to reach maximum strength. Keep this in mind when standing on yesterday's work to lay a few more treads. Treat the stairway delicately for about one week.

This method of stairway building creates an open space underneath for storage. You may want to design a doorway or arch for access to this space.

Once this technique is mastered, there is no limit to where and how you can apply it.

8 GRAVITY SKYLIGHTS

C O M P O N E N T S

THE GRAVITY OPERATED SKYLIGHT IS AN INTEGRAL PART OF THE EARTHSHIP VENTILATION SYSTEM. IT IS THE RESULT OF MANY YEARS OF EVOLUTION OF OPERABLE SKYLIGHTS. THOUGH IT IS VERY SIMPLE IN CONCEPT AND DESIGN, IT HAS MANY IDIOSYNCRASIES THAT ARE CRITICAL TO ITS PERFORMANCE. IF CONSTRUCTED AND INSTALLED PROPERLY, IT WILL LAST A LIFE TIME WITH NO MOTORS OR GEARS TO REPLACE. THIS CHAPTER WILL TAKE YOU THROUGH THIS SKYLIGHT STEP BY STEP IN CONCEPT, CONSTRUCTION, AND MATERIALS.

VENTILATION CONCEPTS

The controlled movement of air through an Earthship aligns with a natural tendency of warm air to rise. Skylights therefore should be in the highest possible places to allow this warmer air to escape if necessary. Fresh air must be allowed to enter in the lowest possible places. This creates a natural air flow bringing outside fresh cooler air in and allowing hotter staler air to leave via a chimney effect. The result is a natural air flow and air exchange throughout the space.

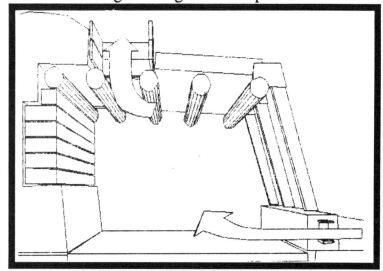

Every "U" module should have this air flow available for individual ventilation, air exchange and cooling.

In extremely hot climates this natural movement of air should be enhanced by extending the skylight box up and providing a black metal surface covered with glazing and sloped south to the sun. This creates much hotter air which rises faster and enhances the suction of cooler air in the lower parts of the Earthship where in-coming air is allowed.

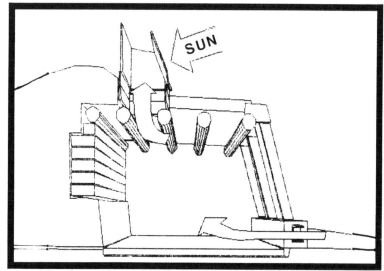

This is called solar enhanced ventilation and is a well used component of buildings in extremely hot climates. Consult an architect, thermal engineer or S.S.A. before building one of these as they require some detailing. At the time of this publication, no existing Earthships have required this apparatus. It is only for extreme desert like conditions.

There is another ventilation variation which can be used in hotter climates where outside air is too hot for comfort. The inlets for incoming air can be taken through the earth before entering the

Earthship. This allows the earth (which stays at about 60 degrees below the surface, see Earthship Vol. I) to cool off the incoming air before it enters the Earthship. The result is a natural air conditioning system which uses no energy and no fans for air movement.

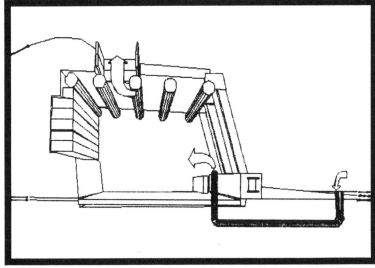

The piping used for this can be 8" or 12" diameter PVC (plastic) pipe with perforations on the bottom side.

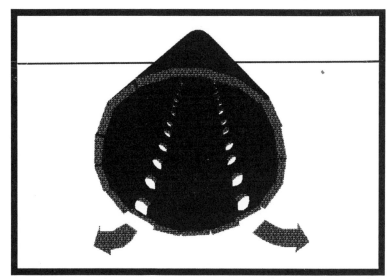

The perforations allow the condensation (brought about by warmer air coming in contact with cooler earth) to escape. This process actually dehumidifies the incoming air. The pipes can come in through the planter. You should have 2 pipes per "U" in addition to an operable window.

The recommended operable window has been updated since Earthship Volume I. We now recommend a lower, smaller, hopper window installed below the front face glass.

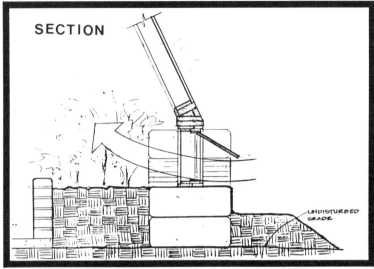

SECTION

UNDISTURBED GRADE

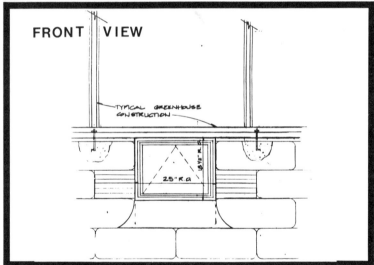

FRONT VIEW

TYPICAL GREENHOUSE CONSTRUCTION

18 1/2" R.O.

25" R.O.

purchase and install. We use a PEACHTREE* metal clad awning window. The rough opening is 18 1/2" x 25" which works exactly with the coursing of #14 tires in the front face stem wall. These tires are about 25" in diameter and 8 1/2" high. The window unit fits into the coursing of the wall as if it were a tire. It does need a third top plate as the two 8 1/2" tires only make 17" in height. Another 1 1/2" is needed for the rough opening

*1 see Appendix, Chapter 8

There are many advantages to this window over the one described in Volume I. It doesn't interrupt the front face glazing with shadows or blockage of sun and view like the one described before. It is also considerably cheaper to

148

This does break the structural integrity of the stem wall somewhat so we advise cement/can void filling on both sides of the stem wall as opposed to the normal mud/can void filling which is used where the stem wall is not interrupted. Be sure to chink around the window tightly with batt insulation. A "bullnose" lath detail (see page 183 Earthship Vol. I) is required when plastering around the window.

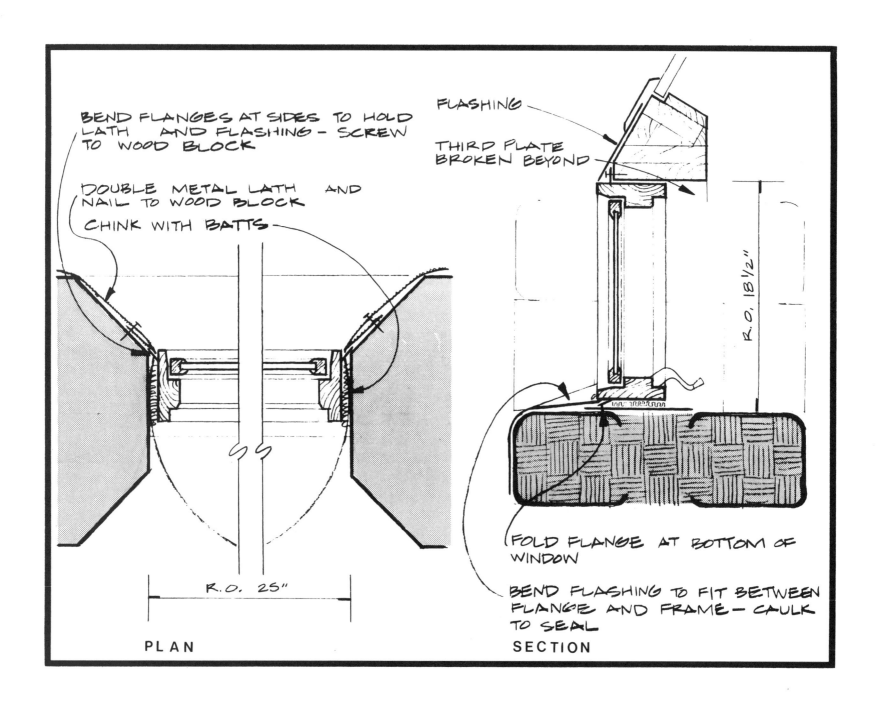

BEND FLANGES AT SIDES TO HOLD
LATH AND FLASHING - SCREW
TO WOOD BLOCK

DOUBLE METAL LATH AND
NAIL TO WOOD BLOCK

CHINK WITH BATTS

FLASHING

THIRD PLATE
BROKEN BEYOND

R.O. 18½"

R.O. 25"

PLAN

FOLD FLANGE AT BOTTOM OF
WINDOW

BEND FLASHING TO FIT BETWEEN
FLANGE AND FRAME - CAULK
TO SEAL

SECTION

150

SKYLIGHT CONSTRUCTION

The skylight is a custom made, operable roof window, counter balanced with weight on a lever arm. It opens by the force of gravity when released and simply pulls shut.

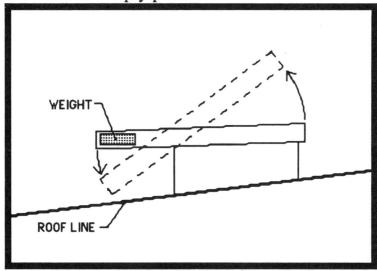

Installation of the initial skylight box (roof opening) is described on pages 114 & 115 of Earthship Volume I. The next step is the glass frame. This frame is made from pressure treated 2x4 stock dimension lumber.

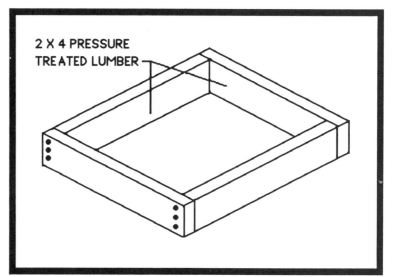

It is sized slightly larger than the skylight box to allow for weather stripping and flashing details.

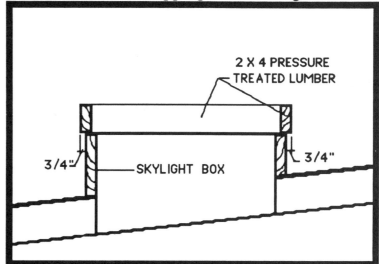

151

The glass frame box now has the lever arm box built around it with pressure treated 2x6 stock. This box also serves as a weather skirt. By locating this box 1-1/4" above the 2x4 glass frame box you form a seat for the glass.

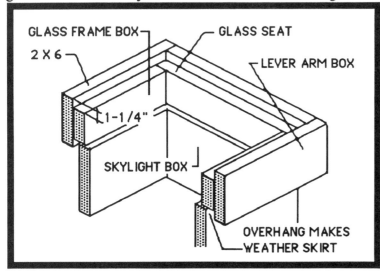

This box is extended to form the lever arm and weight as shown opposite. The length of the lever arm (as well as the weight) varies with the skylight size and weight. A shorter arm means more weight and a longer arm means less weight.

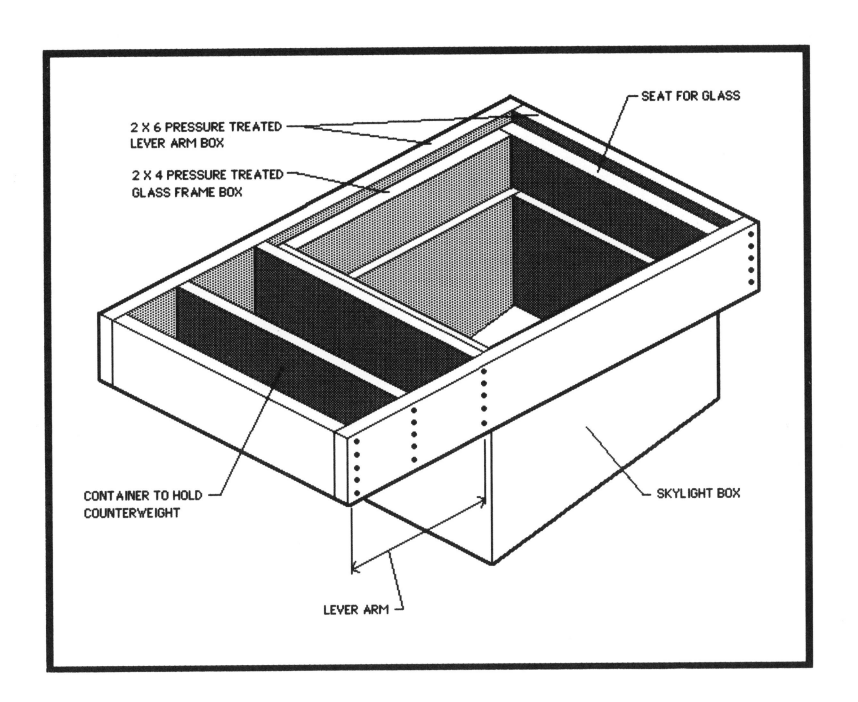

SEAT FOR GLASS

2 X 6 PRESSURE TREATED
LEVER ARM BOX

2 X 4 PRESSURE TREATED
GLASS FRAME BOX

CONTAINER TO HOLD
COUNTERWEIGHT

SKYLIGHT BOX

LEVER ARM

153

Roofing must come up to the top of the skylight box. The 2x6 lever arm box overhangs this roofing for the weather skirt. On top it forms a seat to receive the glass.

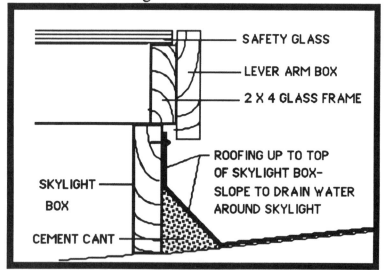

All exposed wood should be pressure treated and/or oiled for protection as wood on a roof takes a lot of abuse.

The glass is a 1-3/16" thick unit made up of three layers of 1/4" safety glass (non-shattering). The use of safety glass is very important since the unit is overhead.

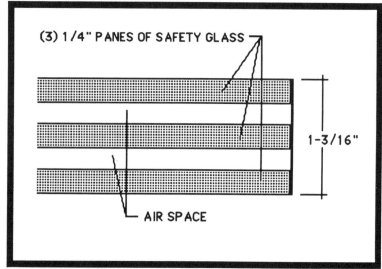

This unit could be made of the new types of glass that are on the market which retain more heat.* In this case it would be double pane and would only be 1" thick. These new types of glass are more expensive and take longer to get. Check with your local glass dealer. The triple paned unit is almost equal in performance and usually easier to obtain. The important factor is that all the pieces of glass be shatter proof for safety. **Remember this glass is over your head.** Wire glass (glass with wire mesh formed inside of it) can be used in cases where hail is a problem.

There are manufactured skylight domes that can be used here. They simply fit over the outside 2x6 skirt.

*2 see Appendix, Chapter 8

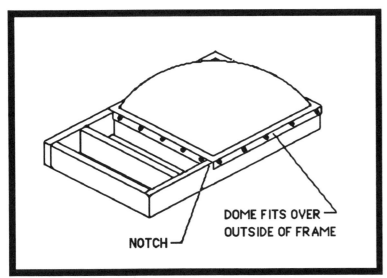

DOME FITS OVER
OUTSIDE OF FRAME

NOTCH

They require a slight notch to be cut in their frame to allow the balance arm to pass through.

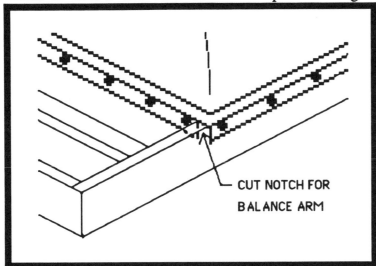

CUT NOTCH FOR
BALANCE ARM

For both cases (manufactured dome or custom glass) **it is best to install the weight in the box after the skylight has been totally**

detailed. This is the only way to get the right amount of weight for the counter balance.

If a regular custom glass unit is used, the unit should be seated on the lid frame in clear butyl caulk and held in with a piece if 2x2 drip edge flashing. Before installing the flashing fill the gap between the glass and the 2x6 with butyl caulk. Fill it solid so the unit will not leak even without the flashing. The glass should be sized so this space is no larger than 1/8".

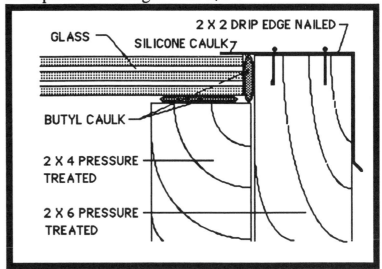

GLASS

2 X 2 DRIP EDGE NAILED

SILICONE CAULK

BUTYL CAULK

2 X 4 PRESSURE
TREATED

2 X 6 PRESSURE
TREATED

The flashing is screwed into the 2x6 lever arm box. The 2x2 drip edge must be sealed to the glass with a generous bead of silicone caulk. The silicone caulk sometimes interacts with the material used to laminate the three panes of glass. Therefore, it can not be used where it touches the laminating material on the edges of the glass unit.

Silicone caulk <u>can</u> be used where it does not touch the edges of the glazing unit.

The 2x2 drip edge comes with a 90 degree bend. This 90 degree bend must be carefully squeezed in to about 70 degrees. Upon installation, it makes a tighter fit when it is forced back to the 90 degree position.

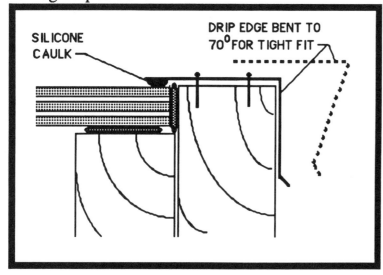

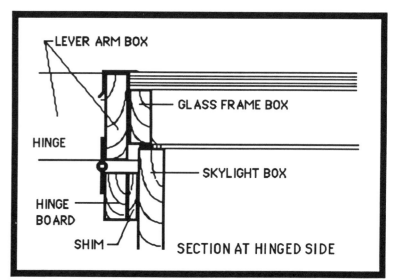

The lid is weather stripped in two places as shown. Foam "stick on" weather striping is stuck on the underneath side of the lid. If it is installed on the box side the sun will destroy it. **This foam must go on before the hinges are installed as it slightly raises the skylight.** If hinges are installed first, the lid will be too tight on the hinge side and not tight enough on the opposite side.

HINGING

The skylight box must be shimmed on the hinge side (usually south) to allow the hinge board to fit flush with the lever arm box. 3" to 4" butt hinges are used - 3 per skylight. Hinges must be installed **after** weather stripping (described later) as the thickness of the weather stripping slightly re-positions the skylight lid.

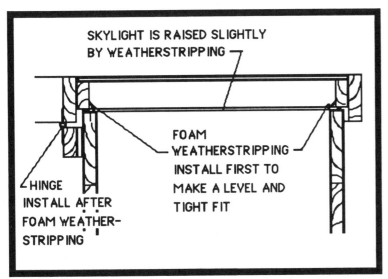

SKYLIGHT IS RAISED SLIGHTLY BY WEATHERSTRIPPING

FOAM WEATHERSTRIPPING INSTALL FIRST TO MAKE A LEVEL AND TIGHT FIT

HINGE INSTALL AFTER FOAM WEATHER-STRIPPING

The other piece of weather stripping mounts inside the lid and fits tight against the box.

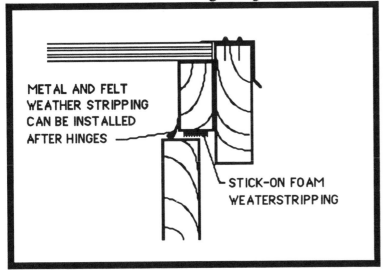

METAL AND FELT WEATHER STRIPPING CAN BE INSTALLED AFTER HINGES

STICK-ON FOAM WEATERSTRIPPING

It can be installed after the hinges. Many types of weather stripping will work for this. The sun does blast this area so the best type is metal and felt neither of which will rot from sun abuse. Some plastics and rubber deteriorate in the sun.

WEIGHTING

The counter balance weight is usually poured concrete. The balance box is detailed as shown to receive the concrete.

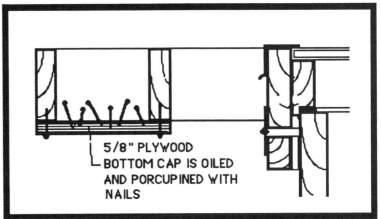

5/8" PLYWOOD BOTTOM CAP IS OILED AND PORCUPINED WITH NAILS

The box is capped on the bottom with 5/8" plywood to hold the concrete. It should be oiled (with linseed oil) and porcupined before pouring in the concrete. The oil is to prevent rotting and the porcupine detail (with 1-1/2" roofing nails) is to hold in the concrete. The weighting must happen after the glass is installed and all detailing is complete. This is to assure an appropriate counter balance weight. Simply pour in the concrete until the weight of the concrete opens the skylight. Shut the skylight. If it opens again by itself you have enough concrete. The concrete will get lighter as it cures so have it a little on the

heavy side. You can adjust it with a rock or two
later. A sheet metal lid should be installed on the
weight box so it won't hold water and rot.

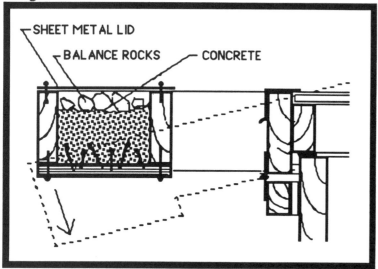

HARDWARE

The skylight is pulled shut with a small cable.
The cable is guided by screw eyes. A turnbuckle
is installed to provide winter tightening. Small
steel rings are used to hook the skylight to lag
screw heads for different positions. A dowel (or
long stick) with a hook on the end is used for
operation. The spring illustrated above is a very
important factor of the hardware. It allows a bit
of tension and stretching to occur so the lid can be
pulled over the lag heads.

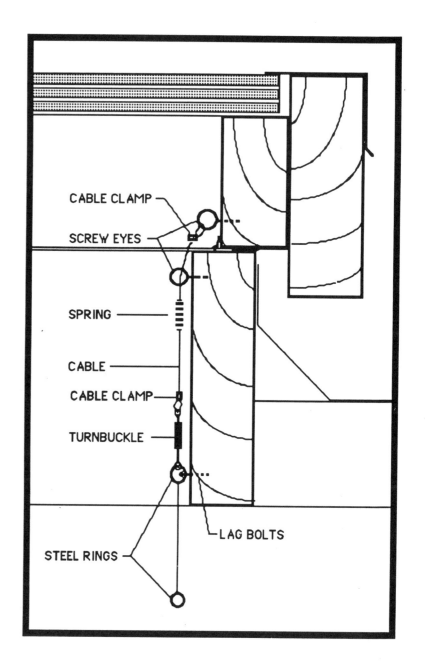

The most common mistake in this hardware installation is that the spring is not heavy duty enough and fatigues. Be sure to get a sturdy, automotive type spring (see Appendix, Chapter 8).

Install the hardware with the turnbuckle open all the way. This will allow tightening later.

A screen can be stapled over the skylight box with a small slit for the guided cable.

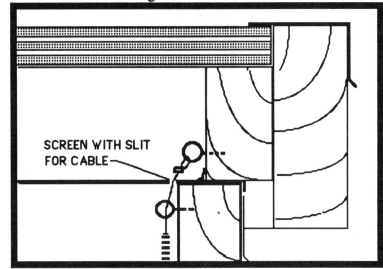

SCREEN WITH SLIT FOR CABLE

The entire skylight should be painted and or oiled for it receives a lot of abuse from the weather on the roof. Flashing should be rubbed with vinegar before painting. This removes the galvanized film so the paint will stay on longer.

The skylight must have a cushion to keep it from banging against the roof. One or two #13 tires are perfect for this.

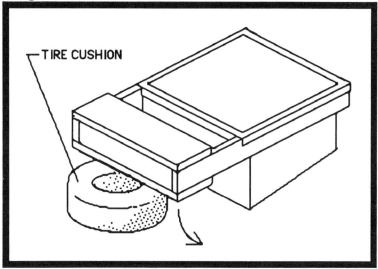

TIRE CUSHION

You now have an operable skylight that will never wear out with two or more open positions and the only energy it uses is the free energy of **GRAVITY.**

APPENDIX

SPRINGS FOR SKYLIGHT
Order from SSA
Box 1041
Taos, NM 87571
(505) 758-9870

PEACHTREE WINDOWS
Model - A2418   Size - 18" x 24"   R.O. - 18 1/2" x 25"
These windows take up to 2 months to get, order
accordingly.
Order from SSA or your local glass dealer.
Box 1041
Taos, NM 87571
(505) 758-9870

DOME SKYLIGHTS
Order from SSA or your local glass dealer.
Box 1041
Taos, NM 87571
(505) 758-9870
Be sure to order triple pane for best heat
retention.

HEAT MIRROR GLASS and LOW E GLASS
See your local glass dealer. There are many
brand names for glass that reduces heat loss.
They are expensive and take a long time to get.

The following photo includes
a SUNFROST refrigerator
(see appendix, Chapter 1)

161

162

9. DOORS AND CABINETS
C O M P O N E N T S

THE SAME BASIC GUIDELINES OF SIMPLICITY, ECONOMY, AND DURABILITY THAT DICTATE THE DESIGN OF THE EARTHSHIP, ALSO APPLY TO THE DESIGN OF EARTHSHIP DOORS AND CABINETS. EACH EARTHSHIP IS FUNDAMENTALLY SIMILAR IN CONCEPT AND GENERAL DESIGN FORMULA, BUT DIFFERENT IN THE FINAL CUSTOM EXECUTION. THIS IS ALSO TRUE OF THE DOOR AND CABINET WORK OF EARTHSHIPS. THEY ARE SIMILAR IN PRINCIPLE YET OPEN TO INDIVIDUAL INTERPRETATION, EXPERIMENTATION AND PERSONAL TASTE. LIKE THE EARTHSHIP ITSELF, THE DOORS AND CABINETS REQUIRE ONLY BASIC TOOLS AND SKILLS THUS MAKING THEM MORE DIRECTLY AVAILABLE TO MORE PEOPLE.

DOOR CONCEPT

Much of today's housing has light, hollow core doors that you can put your foot or fist through. They are cheap and do the job but they are bland and do not shut out much sound. Conventional solid doors are expensive and usually involve major skills and equipment to make. They depend on glue and complicated joints to keep them solid. Still, over time, many doors loosen up and begin to rack or sag and fall apart.

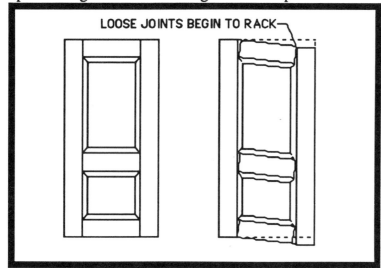

Earthship doors have a plywood core which acts as a solid, structural diaphragm. A wood frame and infill is then installed on either or both visible sides of the diaphragm.

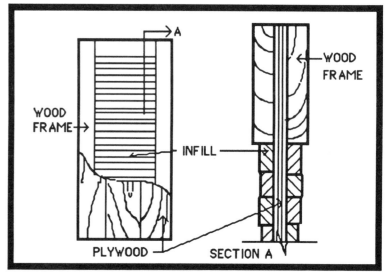

The sandwiched plywood diaphragm makes for an extremely strong door that will never droop or sag and can be filled with almost any material that the maker wishes. Part of the original concept of these doors was to use up various wood scraps from the construction site in the middle infill areas. There are no special tools or skills, such as those involved in dado cuts, tongue and groove, etc., needed to make these doors. The main ingredient, plywood, can be found in any hardware store. These doors are among the most solid, sensible and uniquely beautiful you will see anywhere. They require only a measuring tape, hammer, square and a conventional skill saw.

164

This chapter will discuss four different door types: exterior, interior, cabinet and closet doors. All are similar in design but different in detail. The four types of doors are different in their functions, how they are built and how many sides are covered with decoration - one or both. Whereas closet and cabinet doors need only one finished face, exterior and interior room doors usually have a wooden border and decorative infill on both sides.

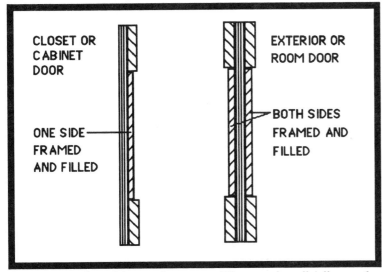

Closet and cabinet doors will require "A" grade plywood on the exposed side. On exterior and room doors both sides of the plywood will be covered so you can use "CD" plywood. Plywood comes in grades as per the quality of the surfaces. "AD" plywood has one good side, "A" and one rough side, "D". This type of plywood is used for closet and cabinet doors with the "A" side exposed on the inside of the closet or cabinet.

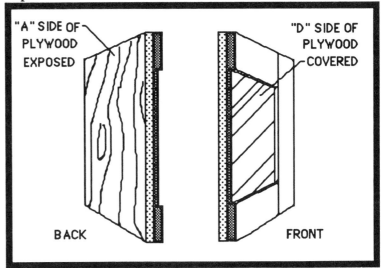

"CD" plywood has two rough sides , the "C" side being slightly better than the other. This plywood is cheaper and used for exterior and interior room doors as they are covered both sides.

CONSTRUCTION

EXTERIOR DOORS

The first step in the construction of any door is to lay a suitable piece of 5/8" plywood against the jamb and trace the opening directly on to the surface of the plywood. Make sure the plywood is pushed tightly against the jamb on all sides as this will determine the width and height of the finished door. Since most jambs (door frames) are rarely perfectly square, this procedure of tracing and fitting the door to the jamb is important. It makes the eventual hanging of the door easier. Label both sides of the plywood. Once you have cut out the plywood diaphragm and checked its fit to the jamb, you can begin to cut and fit the border on to it.

The border is made of 1"x 6" pine, nailed and glued around the perimeter of the plywood core. The bottom piece is 1"x 12" for more durability. This work should be done horizontally on a flat and level work table to insure flatness and ease of construction. This is also done to insure that the door is not constructed in a warped position as it will stay that way. The two vertical border pieces should run flush and continuous from the very top to the very bottom of the door on one side and the horizontal pieces should be continuous on the other side.

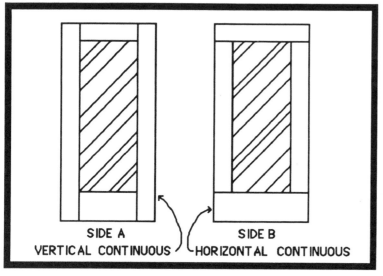

SIDE A
VERTICAL CONTINUOUS

SIDE B
HORIZONTAL CONTINUOUS

This is to avoid the same joint location on both sides of the door making a weak spot. The remaining horizontal and vertical borders should fit between and flush to the continuous borders around the door. The borders of both sides of the door are usually completed first and the infill added later. An exterior door begins with the installation of the outside border. 4d nails are used in a pattern to nail these borders on. Keep the nails 1 1/2" off the bottom to allow for trimming the door for a threshold.

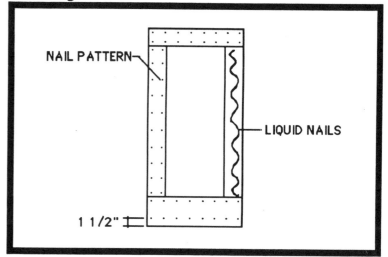

NAIL PATTERN

LIQUID NAILS

1 1/2"

In addition to the 4d nails, use any good exterior carpenters glue or Liquid nails (a type of glue). The 4d nails are spaced a maximum of 8" apart on the exterior to keep the wood from cupping with weather abuse. They are then set and cleated (bent over) to cinch the exterior boards to the plywood in a way that weather abuse can have little effect.

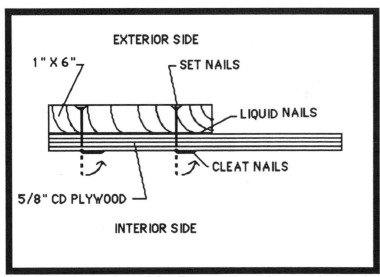

Start the exterior side first. The plywood should be set up on a <u>flat</u> work table with 2x4 shims under it to allow the nails to extend through for cleating. Set them first and then cleat them.

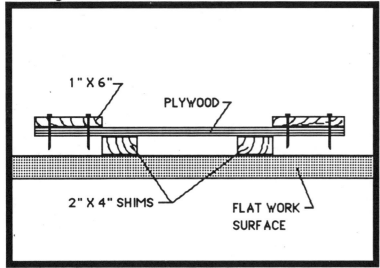

After the exterior wood border has been installed,

flip the door over, cleat the nails and install the border on the opposite side. Remember to run the joints the opposite of how they are on the outside (see diagram previous page). The nails on the inside can't be cleated but remember to use liquid nails or glue. Set the nails in with a nail set. Now you are ready for the infill work.

All the infill work follows the same procedure. Do the outside first. Glue the pieces then set and cleat the nails. Then do the inside and set the nails. It is a good idea to cut and fit all the infill pieces before nailing or gluing any of them. This way your patterns will come out exactly how you want before they are attached.

Sometimes a thick border to frame your "center piece" works well.

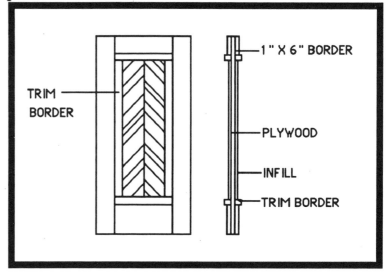

The infill patterns can be anything you can dream up. We have used willow reeds, small aspen poles ripped in half, scrap lumber, etc.

Windows can be added by simply cutting a hole in the plywood the shape of the window you want and trimming out the window as part of the design. Glass is held in with stops both sides just like a regular window. Be sure to seat the glass well in silicone caulk as the door slamming can cause the glass to rattle if it is not seated well.

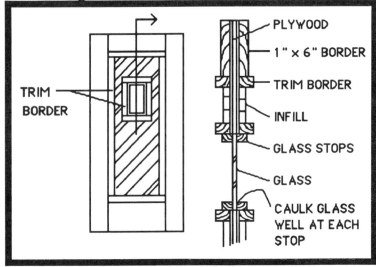

PLYWOOD

1" x 6" BORDER

TRIM BORDER

INFILL

GLASS STOPS

GLASS

CAULK GLASS WELL AT EACH STOP

TRIM BORDER

Following are some examples of exterior doors.

169

Glass Exterior Doors

Glass exterior doors follow all the same procedures. However there are a few detailing options. One way is to detail large glass just like small glass.

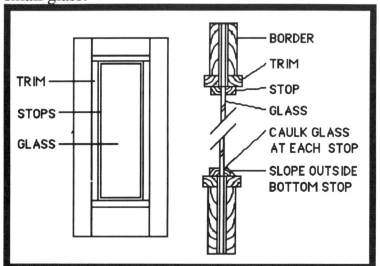

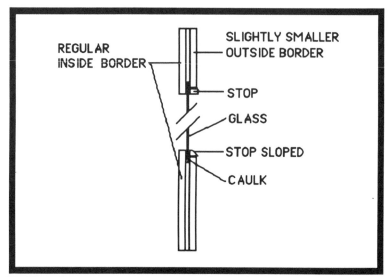

Always seat the glass in a generous caulk bead to avoid rattling. The outside bottom stop should be sloped for water runoff. Caulk the stops against the glass as you install them. The stops are tacked in with small, 3d finish nails.

Another exterior glass door detail incorporates the border 1"x 6" pieces as the stops on the inside. The outside is then stopped with 3/4" x 3/4" stops. Be sure to seat the glass in caulk. Glass doors can be as elaborate as your imagination allows based on this theme.

Following are some examples of glass doors.

170

INTERIOR DOORS

Interior doors follow all the same procedures as exterior doors except in this case it doesn't matter which side you cleat the nails on. On both interior and exterior doors the edges should be sanded smooth so the plywood and frame pieces are all flush and smooth to the touch. Sanding and/or planing is also necessary for final fitting of the door to it s specific opening.

Since interior doors do not require a threshold, the 1 1/2" space before nailing at the bottom (see pages 166 & 167) is not necessary.

Both types of doors should be oiled on both sides with one or two coats of boiled linseed oil cut half and half with mineral spirits. This seals the door and reduces the possibility of any warping before installation. Following are some examples of interior doors.

CLOSET DOORS

Closet doors do not require framing and filling on the closet side. This means you must use a finished plywood (AD) as described on page 165. A smaller sized nail (3d) should be used so the nails will not come through to the finished side of the plywood. Remember to use liquid nails or glue as well.

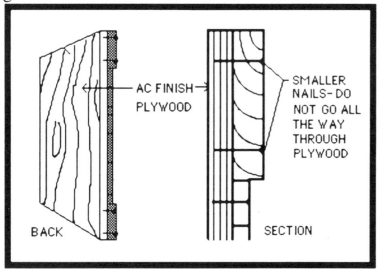

BACK

AC FINISH PLYWOOD

SMALLER NAILS - DO NOT GO ALL THE WAY THROUGH PLYWOOD

SECTION

CABINET DOORS

Cabinet doors follow the same procedure as closet doors with respect to the finished plywood side and the shorter nails. The major difference here is the size. Cabinet doors are smaller so the width of the frame pieces will be smaller. Since cabinet doors are smaller there is a tendency to use plywood with the grain going horizontally. Do not let this happen. Nine times out of ten, doors made this way cup or bow.

On all doors make sure the grain of the plywood is vertical. If you allow the grain to be horizontal the plywood has a tendency to cup or bow.

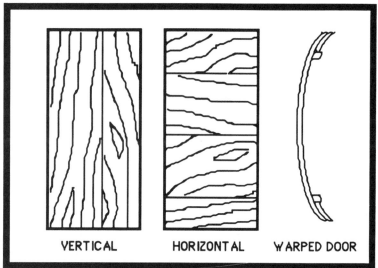

VERTICAL   HORIZONTAL   WARPED DOOR

Following are some examples of cabinet doors.

CABINETS

UPPER WALL CABINETS

The basic look of an Earthship is massive with thick walls and heavy timbers put together in a very simple manner. Cabinets can be built to look just as basic and massive. Light veneer cabinets sometimes look out of place in an Earthship aside from being more difficult and expensive to build. The most visible part of cabinetry is the doors, which you already know how to build. Most upper cabinets in kitchens or bathrooms are simply wood boxes. These boxes are nailed or screwed together out of 2x12 and 2x4 lumber with plywood backs.

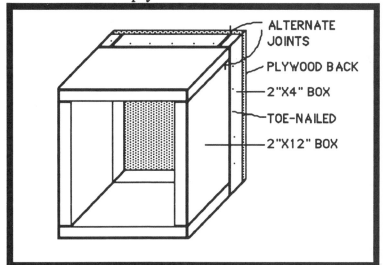

ALTERNATE JOINTS
PLYWOOD BACK
2"X4" BOX
TOE-NAILED
2"X12" BOX

The desired depth of the cabinet is achieved by joining a 2x12 box and a 2x4 box. Note that the joints are alternated - one way on one box and the other way on the second box. This keeps the

177

same joint from happening in both places. Sometimes this is not done if the side or sides of the cabinet are in a prominent place visually. The two boxes can be "toe-nailed" or screwed together as shown below. Toe-nailing can be done neatly in a pattern and set with a nail set. Do more toe-nailing on the top and bottom where it doesn't show.

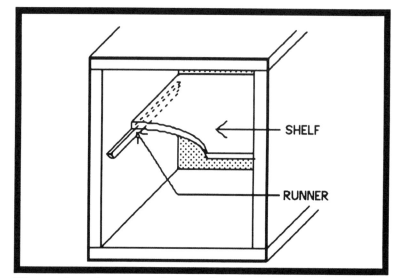

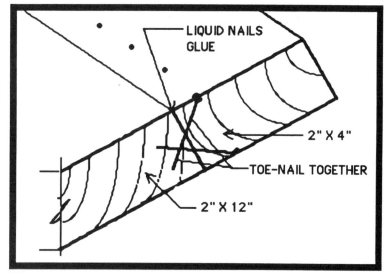

The two boxes should also be glued during this process with liquid nails or carpenter's glue. Make sure the unit is square and then nail on a plywood back.

Shelves can be added as desired on 3/4" x3/4" runners as shown. The shelf runners, which are nailed into both boxes, can also be used to help hold the two boxes together.

There is also an alternative method of putting together the same cabinet which eliminates the need for toe-nailing. The same pieces can be put together in a staggered arrangement the very nature of which integrally connects the boxes. This is a little more diffucult to assemble.

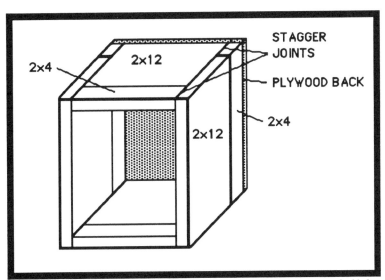

Since the front of the cabinet is the most visible, the front edge is usually sanded and sometimes routed to give it a round, soft effect. The doors are then set inside this front edge and framed by the structure of the cabinet itself.

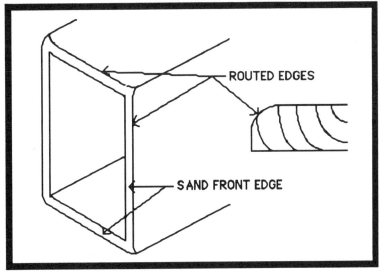

179

The best way to mount the cabinet or cabinets on a tire wall is to first cover the mounting area with a 3/4" piece of plywood screwed (in many places) to the tires.

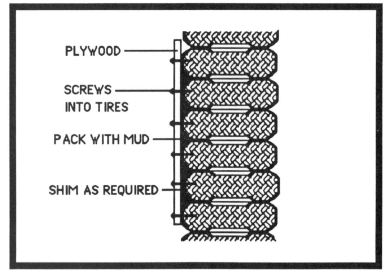

This piece of plywood must be shimmed into a true plumb and level position as the tires are not always perfectly plumb and in plane. Be sure to fill and pack the tires out to a plane first (see Earthship Vol I, page 175). Regular screws will hold into the front edge of the tires. Be sure to use a lot of them. Make sure they are long enough to go through the plywood and the rubber and be sure to hit tires, not mud fill. If you plan ahead, you can lay in wood blocking where the cabinets will go and have a solid wood block to screw the plywood into.

Now the cabinet unit can be screwed into this plywood mounting surface. Cabinets have also been hung from vigas or beams and attached directly to wood blocking placed strategically in the tire walls as shown below.

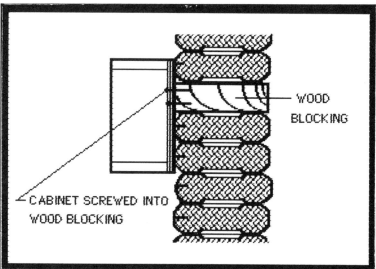

This method requires you to know where this blocking is going to be and install it as the tire wall is constructed.

COUNTERTOP CABINETS
The same box type unit is used here only the units are usually deeper and require a 2x12, a 2x4 and a second 2x12 to get the required depth for lower counter cabinets. 2x4's are used on the top of this box as the plywood top will ultimately make the top solid.

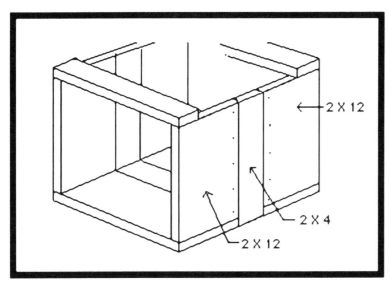

There is also the addition of a toe kick space at the bottom. This can be achieved by making a small 2x4 box recessed in from the front of the unit about 3 1/2".

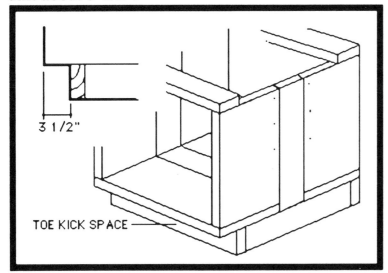

This raises the unit up off of the floor and provides a toe kick space.

For countertops use a double layer of 3/4" plywood if you plan to do tile work. This gives you a thick 1 1/2" edge to accommodate tile details.

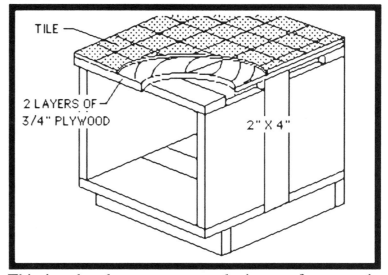

This is why the top structural pieces of your unit can be eliminated except for a 2x4 at the front and back as the plywood takes over the job of the other wood.

If you want a wood counter top, have a carpenter dowel and glue the countertop together for you out of dried 1 1/2" thick lumber to your required size specifications. It can be screwed in from the bottom to your simple wood box unit.

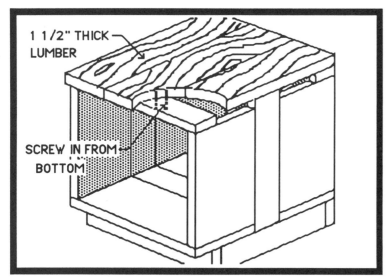

These units also have plywood backs and in most cases a back splash which is simply a 2x6 on edge screwed into the top.

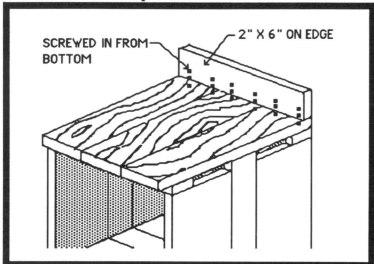

This is the basic idea of Earthship cabinets - **wood boxes with pretty doors.**

Like the Earthship itself, this method can be elaborated upon relative to ones own particular skills and budget. The accompanying diagram illustrates a somewhat more refined and difficult version of this same concept.

The following photographs illustrate some of the many examples of these kind of cabinets.

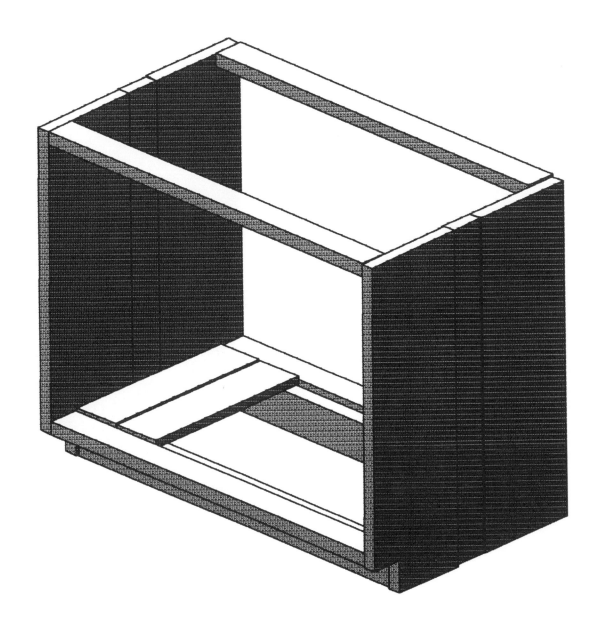

The upper and lower cabinets are simply a series of individual boxes built as described earlier in the chapter. When a drawer bank is desired, the initial box is built the same way. Drawers are then built in a conventional manner to fit into the box. Have a carpenter help you with drawers.

APPENDIX

Liquid Nails
> Available at most hardware stores
> Macco Adhesive, Glidden Co.
> Cleveland, Ohio 44115

Nails
> "d" is the symbol for "penny" - a "3d"
> nail is a "3 penny" nail.

Plywood
> It comes in 1/2", 5/8", 3/4", and 1"
> thickness. Sides range from A to D - "A"
> is a finished side and "D" is a rough side.
> "X" means exterior glue is used. Most
> regular doors use 5/8" CDX. Cabinet and
> closet doors use 1/2" ADX so the "A"
> side can be exposed.

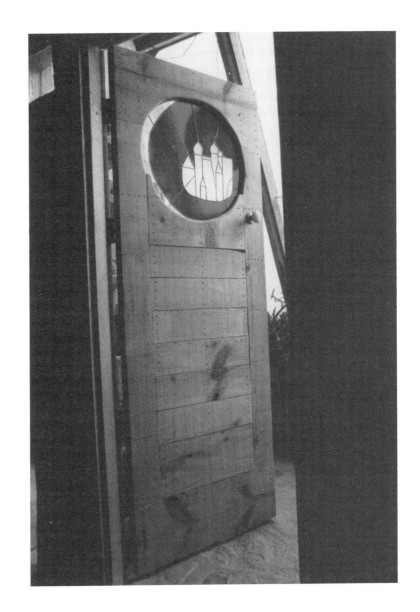

186

10. BATHTUBS, SHOWERS, VANITIES

MOST EARTHSHIP BATHROOMS ARE PLACED RIGHT UP AGAINST THE SOLAR FRONT FACE AND ARE FILLED WITH PLANTS AND MOISTURE. IN THIS SITUATION, THE BATHROOM BECOMES A WHOLE DIFFERENT EXPERIENCE FROM CONVENTIONAL BATHROOMS. IT BECOMES A CAPTURED EXTERIOR GARDEN TYPE SPACE. BOTH THE SHAPE OF THE SPACE AND THE NATURE OF THE SPACE DESERVE SOMETHING MORE THAN WHAT CONVENTIONAL BATHROOM FIXTURES HAVE TO OFFER. FOR THIS REASON WE HAVE DEVELOPED METHODS OF SCULPTING TUBS, SHOWERS, PLANTERS AND VANITIES OUT OF THE SAME MATERIALS THAT THE BATHROOM WALLS ARE MADE OF - CANS AND CEMENT. THIS ALLOWS YOU TO BOTH DESIGN AND BUILD YOUR OWN FANTASY INDOOR/OUTDOOR BATHING SPACE.

188

The previous photo illustrates the sculpted effect of tub and planter all custom built of the same materials with stucco and tile finish. We will take these units one at a time and discuss the procedures involved in their construction. Then, how you sculpt them together is up to your own imagination.

VANITIES

The vanity is a wooden door frame laid into two can walls on either side. The first step is to make the door frame out of 2x4 stock with a toe kick space as in the kitchen cabinet design in chapter 8.

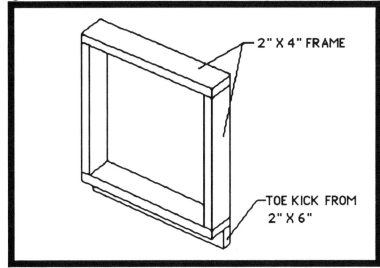

The toe kick is also made from a 2x4 screwed or nailed to the bottom of the door frame box.

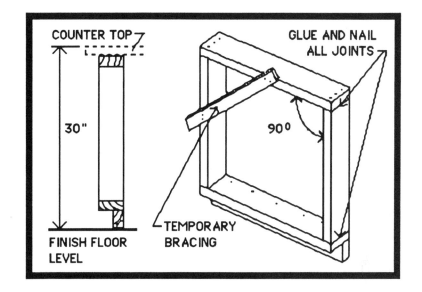

Sink counters are usually about 30" high. After you deduct the toe kick and a couple of inches for the top detail, you are left with about 25" for the overall height of the door frame. The width is your desired width of the overall vanity minus 5" either side for the can walls. Make sure the frame is square and braced in a square condition with a diagonal. Also notice that the top and bottom pieces are continuous. This is stronger. Glue the joints with Liquid Nails* or carpenters glue in addition to nailing or screwing.

* 1 See Appendix, Chapter 10

189

Now the frame is positioned on the floor where you want the cabinet. If the finished floor is not in yet, you have to prop the frame up to where the bottom of the toe kick is on finish floor. Metal lath tabs should be installed on either side of the cabinet frame as described on page 166 of Earthship Volume I.

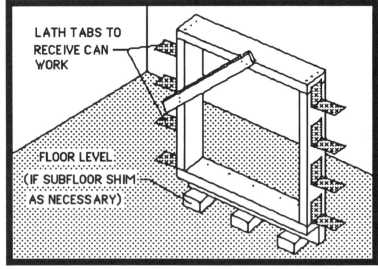

These tabs will hold the can work to the frame. Now you are ready to lay the can work on either side of the frame. Refer to Earthship Volume I, page 158-160 for can laying pointers. Lay the cans up to about 1 1/2" from being flush with the height of the wooden frame. The can work is what stabilizes the door frame. An attachment to the floor is not necessary.

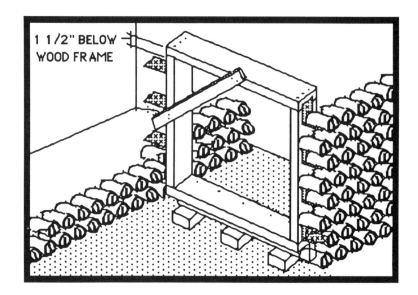

Now you are ready to put the plywood top on. The plywood can be 5/8"cdx (exterior) plywood if the cabinet is fairly small. If it is large, make the plywood 3/4". The plywood is anchored to the can work with the porcupine technique (as described in Chapter 7). Small roofing nails are nailed along the edges then the plywood is set in an inch and a half thick patty of cement on top of the can walls.

PORCUPINE NAILS TO
SET IN CEMENT

This makes the plywood set flat on the surface of the door frame. Notice that the plywood is set back about 1 1/2" from the front of the frame as well as the sides of the can walls. This allows the plaster to achieve a rounded effect later. The plywood can be nailed or screwed to the top of the door frame.

Now cut the hole for the sink to fit into. All sinks are different sizes so you must have you sink on hand for this step.

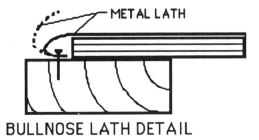

METAL LATH

BULLNOSE LATH DETAIL

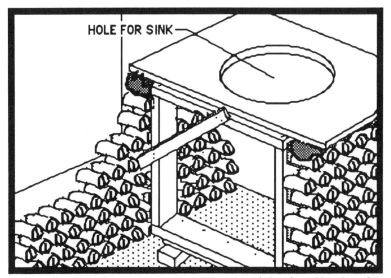

HOLE FOR SINK

The plywood must be covered with 6 mil plastic and metal lath to receive plaster. Make sure the metal lath extends and overlaps well onto the can wall.

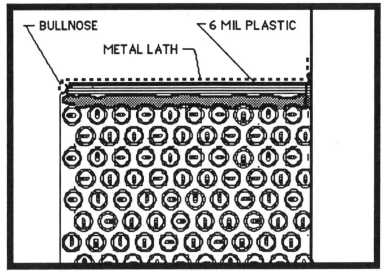

BULLNOSE — 6 MIL PLASTIC
METAL LATH

Use a bullnose lath detail in the front.

191

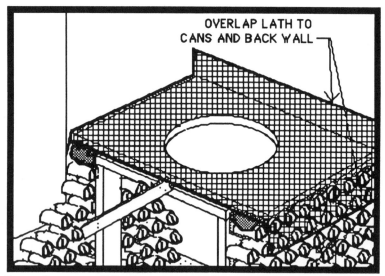

OVERLAP LATH TO
CANS AND BACK WALL

Lap the metal lath up onto the wall in the back as well. Do not allow any breaks in the metal lath as a crack will occur at this location. A bullnose lath detail must also happen around the door on either side in order to anchor the plaster to the door frame.

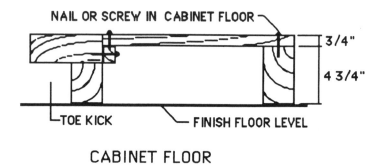

NAIL OR SCREW IN CABINET FLOOR

3/4"

4 3/4"

TOE KICK   FINISH FLOOR LEVEL

CABINET FLOOR

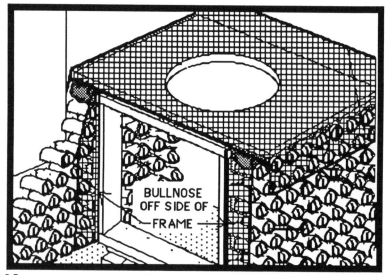

BULLNOSE
OFF SIDE OF
FRAME

Now you are ready to plaster. First a scratch coat. This should be a mix of one part portland cement to three parts plaster sand with engineering fibers*. Plaster the unit inside and out.

A ledger strip should be installed in the back of the bottom of the cabinet to receive the floor of the cabinet. This piece should be installed 3/4" below the bottom of the cabinet door frame as these two pieces together receive the 1x6 floor installed later. This ledger strip can be glued to a finish floor with Liquid Nails or porcupined (see page 190 this chapter or Chapter 7) to a small cement patty if the floor is not in yet.

*2 see Appendix, Chapter 10

192

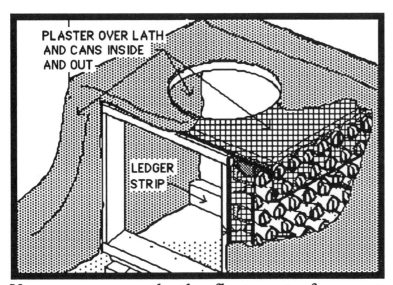

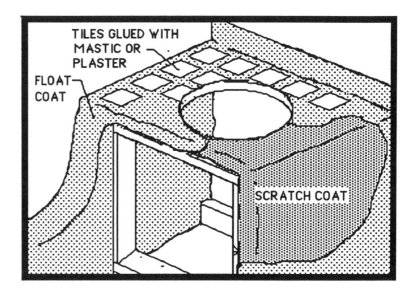

You can now apply the float coat of cement plaster using the same mix. See a local plaster contractor for plastering hints and consult Chapter 9 of Earthship Volume 1. Now tiles can be installed in any pattern you want. Keep them away from the rounded edges. Let your pattern occur only on the flat surface.

Tiles are glued down with regular tile mastic or a rich mix (1 cement to 2 sand) of regular plaster. If you use mastic, make sure your cement has cured a couple of days first. If you use a cement mix make sure you wet the tiles and the counter surface before laying them. Don't let the mastic or the cement "glue" get too thick and elevate your tiles too much. The next layer is stucco which will crack when applied too thick. Elevated tiles require a thick stucco coat.

Sometimes the sink is installed with the tiles as if it were a tile. This requires cutting the tiles around the sink It can also be siliconed down last. This is easiest. Different sinks require different methods of installation. It is best to get a sink with faucet holes then it will not be necessary to make faucet holes in the tile work.

The stucco is now applied in a similar manner to the plaster. The real art in stucco work is knowing how to float it to a smooth surface so it won't be scratchy. You let it slightly set up and then "polish" it with a firm wet sponge or a plaster float from a building supply store. Work the stucco in around your tiles to grout them.

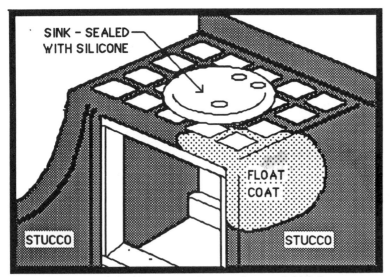

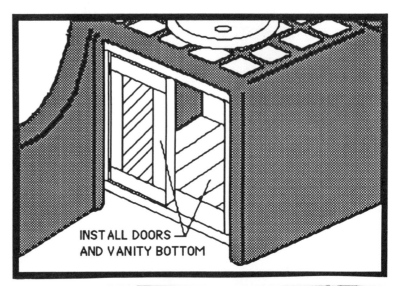

Stucco grouted tiles require at least 1/4" between tiles. Anything less will cause the stucco to crack. Clean the tile immediately as dried stucco is very hard to get off. Keep polishing the tiles with damp and dry rags until they look just like you want them to look.

Stucco can be cleaned with a brush and cleanser and will give you a finish that will last forever. Your stucco should be worked until it is fairly smooth to avoid a scratchy surface. If a local plaster contractor has any experience with stucco, discuss its application with him as stucco takes a little practice to get good at.

Now you can install the floor deck of your cabinet as well as a door as per Chapter 9.

196

BATHTUBS

Bathtubs are started simply by drawing the shape on the floor or subfloor. This is a guide for roughing in the drain. If you are not familiar with plumbing, have a plumber do your rough in. If a grey water system is used, the drain needs no vent or trap. This makes it very easy to rough in the drain pipe and head it toward your grey water planter (see Chapter 3). A plumber will want to put in a vent and trap. Have him read Chapter 3 so he will understand what you want. Code may still require a vent and trap. It can be done but avoid it if possible since it is an unnecessary expense. Next, establish the location of the finish bottom of the tub and install a flush finish drain plug*. Now lay a can wall in the shape of the tub you want to the height you want.

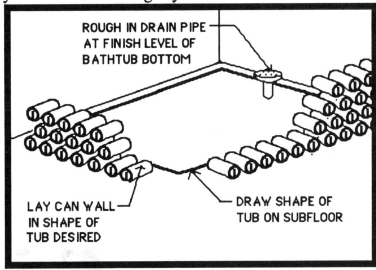

ROUGH IN DRAIN PIPE
AT FINISH LEVEL OF
BATHTUB BOTTOM

LAY CAN WALL
IN SHAPE OF
TUB DESIRED

DRAW SHAPE OF
TUB ON SUBFLOOR

*3 see Appendix, Chapter 10

The rough-in plumbing for the water supply should happen now. If it occurs in an aluminum can wall of your bathroom it can be attached to that wall. Slightly dent in that can work to allow this rough-in copper pipe to recess somewhat into the wall. The Moen Company* now has fixtures that can be serviced from the front so typical pipe chases are not required. The following diagram and photo shows this Moen fixture recessed into the plastered can wall.

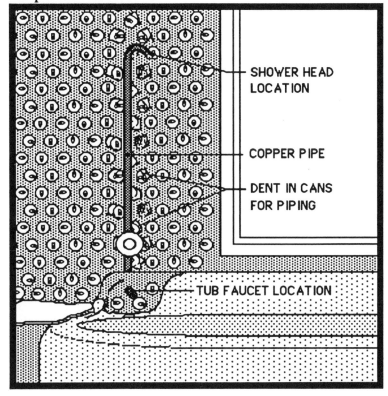

SHOWER HEAD
LOCATION

COPPER PIPE

DENT IN CANS
FOR PIPING

TUB FAUCET LOCATION

*4 see Appendix, Chapter 10

Now take some slightly damp dirt and shape the bottom of the tub to fit your own body or imagination.

Sculpt it and drape it up to the can wall and then tamp it down well.

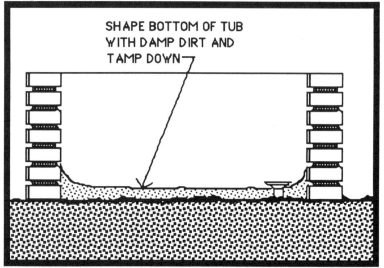

SHAPE BOTTOM OF TUB
WITH DAMP DIRT AND
TAMP DOWN

Cover this dirt with 6 mil plastic and cover that with metal lath. Lap the lath up onto the can wall.

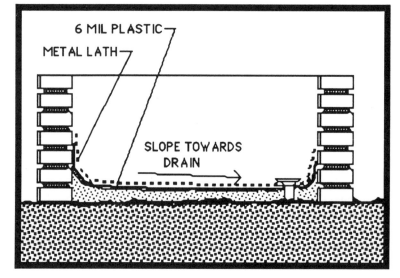

6 MIL PLASTIC
METAL LATH

SLOPE TOWARDS
DRAIN

Be sure to keep a slope going towards your drain. Also keep this work about 1 1/2" below the drain to allow for a 3 coat plaster job.

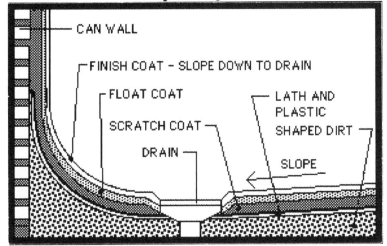

Now apply a scratch coat of 1 cement to 3 sand mixed with engineering fibers* and plaster the entire tub inside and out. Scratch it well to receive the next coat. Next apply a float coat of the same mix. Get the shape you want with this coat. Tiles can be installed after this float coat wherever and however you want. It is important to realize that the inner tub must have a smooth finish coat of some kind whereas the walls and outer tub can be stucco to match the rest of the room and vanity. This may influence your tile work as you may want to use the tiles to separate the two materials.

*4 see Appendix, Chapter 10

After tiles are installed (see discussion for vanities) the tub can be stuccoed anywhere except for the inner water holding part. Be advised that stucco finishes should never have cold joints between work done in different work sessions. You must stucco to a corner or an obvious stopping place. If you stucco part one day and part the next day you will have a crack between the two days work. The inner tub can now be plastered with a smooth plaster using fine sand and smooth troweling. The best final finish for this plaster is an acrylic material made by one of the stucco companies*. This acrylic material is basically painted on and holds up better than anything else we have tried. It comes in all colors and is expensive but you don't need much. Some people have done their whole bathroom with this finish, however, it is difficult to use around tiles.

SHOWERS

Shower spaces can be built with can walls, tiled, plastered, and stuccoed similar to the previous discussion on bathtubs. Often glass blocks are used in shower spaces to add light. A floor lip (made of cans) is also a good idea.

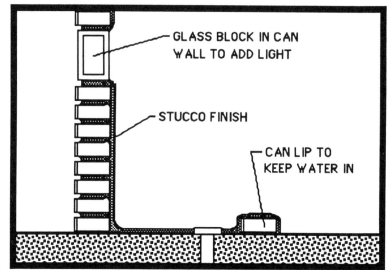

The procedures are all similar to other can wall and plastering discussions. Closed in shower stalls are not necessary and seldom used in this type of bathroom as the whole bathroom is full of plants and waterproof. You can literally hose down your bathroom. This requires a floor drain into a greywater planter (see Chapter 3). In fact it is best not to contain your water in a conventional shower stall as the plants love it. An Earthship shower needs only a light definition of space. Let your imagination take you into the experience and out of plumbing catalogs.

*5 see Appendix, Chapter 10

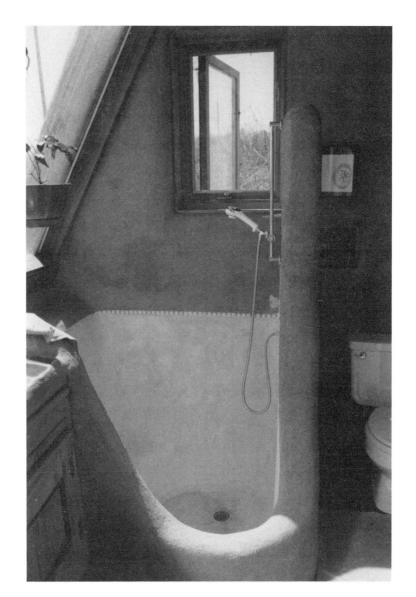

APPENDIX

Faucets
Made by the Moen Company - see your plumber.

Engineering Fibers
Fibermesh Company
4019 Industry Drive
Chattanooga, TN 37416

Stucco
El Rey
4100 Broadway SE
Albuquerque, NM 87105
(505) 873-1180

Acrylic (Tinted Polymer Based Finish)
El Rey
4100 Broadway SE
Albuquerque, NM 87105
(505) 873-1180

Drain for Bathtub
Roman Drain
Order from SSA
Box 1041, Taos, NM 87571
(505) 758-9870

Liquid Nails
Macco Adhesive
Glidden Company
Cleveland, Ohio 44115

204

11. CAN DOMES AND VAULTS
C O M P O N E N T S

THE IDEA OF BUILDING WITH RECYCLED MATERIALS STARTED IN 1970 WITH BUILDINGS MADE OF STEEL CANS. THIS WAS BEFORE ALUMINUM CANS WERE MADE. MANY CAN BUILDINGS WERE BUILT USING VARIOUS TECHNIQUES. AT FIRST THE CANS WERE USED AS INFILL PANEL WALLS IN A POST AND BEAM STRUCTURE. SOON WE REALIZED THAT THE CAN WALLS THEMSELVES COULD BE USED AS BEARING WALLS AND THIS LED TO THE CONTRUCTION OF DOMES, VAULTS, ARCHES ETC. ALL THE CAN BUILDINGS BUILT WERE SUCCESSFUL STRUCTURES, HOWEVER, IN THE MID SEVENTIES WE BEGAN LOOKING FOR WAYS TO BUILD THERMAL MASS INTO BUILDINGS FOR THE PURPOSE OF STABILIZING TEMPERATURES. BECAUSE WE WERE ALREADY BUILDING WITH CANS, WE FOUND OURSELVES IN THE FRAME OF MIND TO SEE THE POSSIBILITY OF USING TIRES FOR BUILDING. ONCE WE TRIED TIRES RAMMED WITH EARTH FOR STRUCTURE AND THERMAL MASS WE SAW THAT WE HAD A METHOD THAT COULD NOT BE MATCHED BY CANS OR ANY CONVENTIONAL MATERIAL IN TERMS OF THE AMOUNT OF THERMAL MASS THAT COULD BE OBTAINED BY THE STRUCTURE ITSELF. THIS PUT AN END TO BUILDINGS MADE TOTALLY OF CANS. HOWEVER, FOR MINOR WALLS LIKE CLOSETS, BATHROOMS, OR ANY INFILL AREAS, THE CAN TECHNIQUES WE HAD EVOLVED OVER THE YEARS PROVED TO BE IDEAL. WE ARE, THEREFORE, PRESENTING THE METHODS USED FOR CAN CONSTRUCTION IN THIS CHAPTER IN MORE DEPTH THAN THE CAN LAYING DISCUSSED IN EARTHSHIP VOLUME I. AS CANS CONTINUE TO BE AN IMPORTANT FACTOR IN EARTHSHIP CONSTRUCTION. THE DOMES, VAULTS AND ARCHES CAN BE USED AS SPECIAL SPACES IN MORE ELABORATE EARTHSHIP DESIGNS. THEY CAN ALSO BE USED TO CREATE A LABYRINTH OF SPACES ABOVE GROUND IN A TEMPERATE CLIMATE AND BELOW GROUND LEVEL IN AN EXTREMELY HOT OR COLD CLIMATE. CANS ARE VERY VERSATILE AND ARE AN EASY WAY TO DO ALMOST ANYTHING IN AN EARTHSHIP THAT ISN'T ALREADY DONE WITH TIRES. THE INFORMATION PRESENTED IN THIS CHAPTER WILL OFFER YOU A *PALLET* OF TECHNIQUES TO SUPPLEMENT THE BASIC TIRE STRUCTURE OF YOUR EARTHSHIP.

CAN PANEL WALLS

This building technique is structured with a typical post and beam network of concrete, steel or wood as shown in the diagram opposite. Post and beam is a standard structural system and can be designed for any size or height of building. In this case it is simply infilled with insulated panels made of aluminum cans. Almost any type of container (steel or aluminum cans and/or bottles) can be used for the infill panel. The cement to sand ratio is 1to4 as the can wall panels are not structural.. Regular portland cement should be used, not masonry cement and concrete sand should be used, not plaster sand. Refer to page 158 of Earthship Volume I for can laying techniques.

Four inch thick rigid foam panels* provide the necessary insulative qualities for the wall (R-30). The air spaces in the containers either side of the foam panel make the insulative qualities of the overall wall a little better. The foam panel is installed between the columns first. It should be tacked or propped up in a vertical plumb position. The masonry work on either side is laid up against it. The inside and outside masonry should be tied together with small strips of metal lath going through the foam. The masonry work must be allowed to set up briefly after about 2-3 feet in height.

*1 see Appendix, Chapter 11

This will avoid bulging of the panels. Recommended maximum panel size is 10'-0" high by 14'-0" long. Any larger size could get expansion cracks.

The outside course of the panels can be designed to bypass the columns or to butt them squarely leaving the column exposed.

If the building is to be plastered, the panel should be made of cans with the mouth holes out to receive the plaster. No stucco netting or other preparation is necessary to plaster over cans, however, any exposed wood or other materials should be treated properly (wrapped in plastic and covered with metal lath) before plastering. The panels do not have to be plastered. We have developed a technique we call "grooming". We rub cement into the joints between the cans after the initial masonry work is laid and set up. We then rub the cement off of the cans or bottles and polish them with a cloth. The cement can also be sprayed off the cans or bottles with a fine mist from a hose this leaves exposed cans in a matrix of cement and can look very interesting if executed well. This technique also opens up the possibilities of bottle mosaic work with the can work, etc.

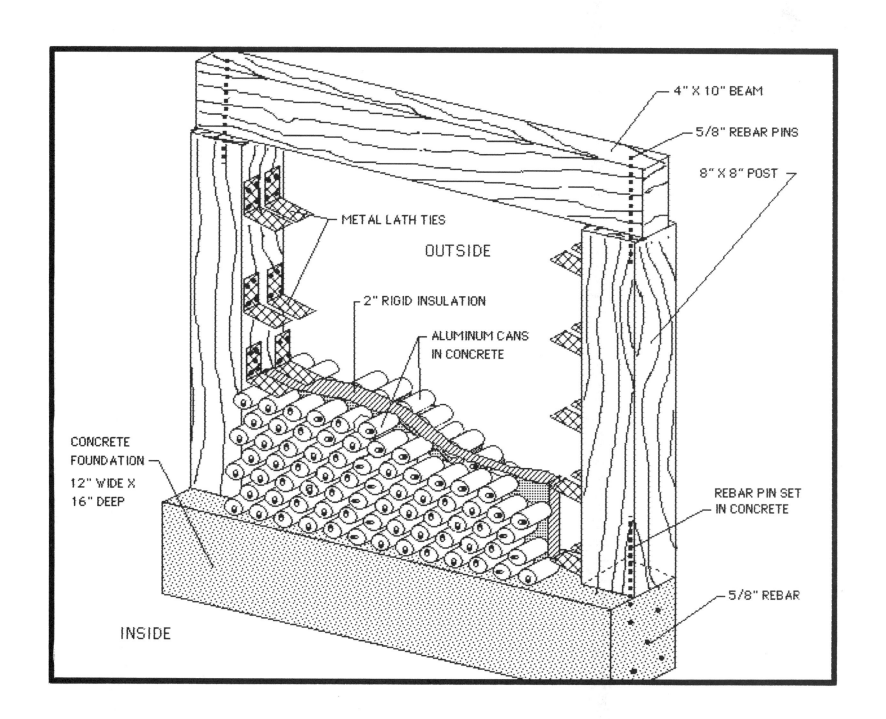

4" X 10" BEAM

5/8" REBAR PINS

8" X 8" POST

METAL LATH TIES

OUTSIDE

2" RIGID INSULATION

ALUMINUM CANS
IN CONCRETE

CONCRETE
FOUNDATION
12" WIDE X
16" DEEP

REBAR PIN SET
IN CONCRETE

5/8" REBAR

INSIDE

207

208

If the panels are not to be plastered, the joints between the columns and the panels as well as between the beams and panels should be made weather proof. An architect or builder should be consulted here as this initial detail can be handled in many ways. It depends on the material being used for the post and beam network.

Mortar techniques vary with the panel material used. In any case, the mortar should be firm not loose. When pressing a can into the mortar the cylindrical can should be crimped to create a sharp edge. This allows the can to be layed with less pressure. Mortar should remain recessed from the outside face of the cans. If it oozes out you are probably using too much or else the mortar is too wet. The cans or bottles should never touch each other. The panels can be groomed, plastered, painted, or left rough. Cans should be laid a minimum of 3/4" apart. This system has passed building codes and been approved for bank financing everywhere it has been used.

210

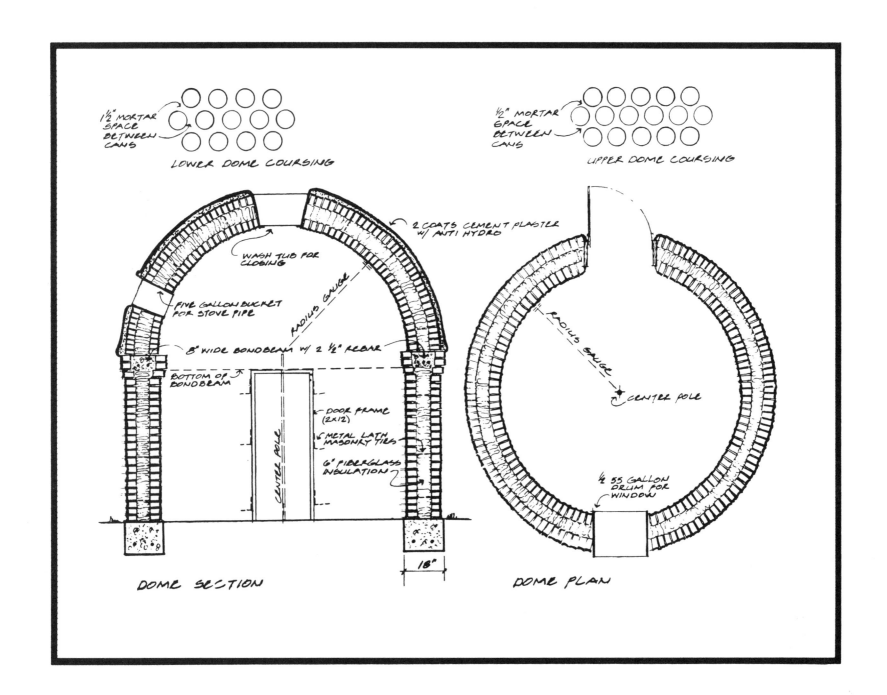

½" MORTAR SPACE BETWEEN CANS

LOWER DOME COURSING

½" MORTAR SPACE BETWEEN CANS

UPPER DOME COURSING

2 COATS CEMENT PLASTER w/ ANTI HYDRO

WASH TUB FOR CLOSING

FIVE GALLON BUCKET FOR STOVE PIPE

RADIUS GAUGE

8" WIDE BONDBEAM w/ 2 ½" REBAR

BOTTOM OF BONDBEAM

CENTER POLE

DOOR FRAME (2x12)

METAL LATH MASONRY TIES

6" FIBERGLASS INSULATION

18"

DOME SECTION

RADIUS GAUGE

CENTER POLE

½ 55 GALLON DRUM FOR WINDOW

DOME PLAN

212

ALUMINUM CAN DOMES

Aluminum can domes have been built using a similar can laying technique to that used in the panel wall system. The drawing opposite illustrates the most popular dome which is actually a hemisphere on top of a cylinder. Can masonry is not limited to the hemisphere. Ellipse domes, vaults, and structural arches of all types have been successfully built. An entire home can be built using a series of domes connected by vaulted hallways.

THE DOUBLE DOME

The foundation depends on location. It should go down to the frost line as in conventional construction. However, If the dome is buried for insulative reasons the foundations would already be well below the surface and need only be 12" deep with two half inch rebars continuous. The can work is then laid on top of the foundation. This can work is structural so use a mortar mix of 1 cement to <u>3 sand</u> with engineering fibers*. The amount of water added is very important. Too much water and the mortar is loose. The wall will fall apart as it is being built. Too little water and the mortar is too dry. The cans will have to be forced into it. Find the right consistency to hold the wall together yet still allow the cans to push easily into the cement. (Refer to page 158 of

*2 see Appendix, Chapter 11

Earthship Volume I).

The spaces between cans in a dome vary. The lower courses of the dome want to have more cement for more strength and mass while the upper courses should have less cement for lighter weight. Therefore, the spaces between the cans on the lower courses should be a minimum of 1-1/2" while in the upper courses a minimum of 1/2" should be used.

The coursing can only be laid up 2 or 3 feet in height at a time. The mortar must be allowed to set up before going any further. As the dome begins to curve in and the joints get smaller (1-1/2" decrease to 1/2") the slope of the cans will only allow 2 or 3 courses at a time. Near the end, the cans are almost vertical and only one course can be applied at a time. Finally at the very end only a few cans at a time can be laid. No forms are needed because the aluminum cans are so light that the stickiness of the mortar will hold them up even in a vertical position. Near the end you may want to add a shovel full of masonry cement to the regular mixture to make it even stickier and which will help hold the cans in the vertical position.

214

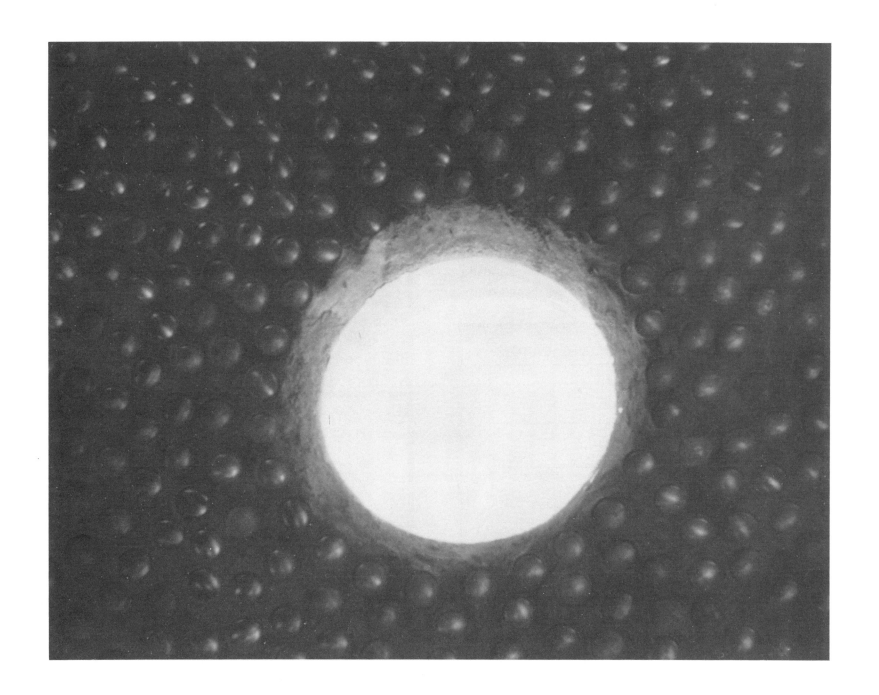

Since the dome is just a circle on the ground, it can be laid out simply by driving a stake in the ground with a nail in the top of it and striking a radius with a string or heavy cord for the desired diameter. We suggest you try a small diameter of 8-10 feet first. We do not recommend domes of over 20'-0" in diameter. The dome illustrated is a simple hemisphere and the layout radius for the cylinder part can be used as a gauge for the dome itself. The radius cord should be attached to a perfectly plumb pole or pipe which is the desired height of the cylinder. The cylinder is gauged by rotating the cord around the pole, raising it as you go up. Keep it level to the horizontal.

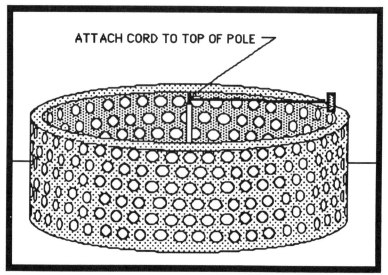

Since you are rotating from a point rather than a pole now your string will form a hemisphere. A little wood handle on the end of the cord is helpful in using it as a gauge.

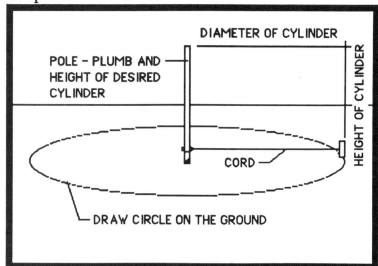

When you get to the beginning of the hemisphere you attach the cord to the top of the pole and keep using it in the same way.

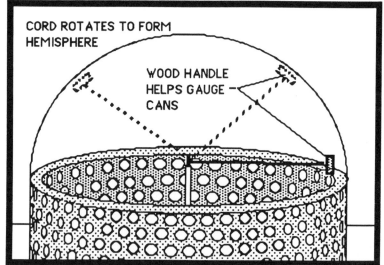

All work should be gauged after every course.

216

Entrances for this structure can be made with standard wood frames (see Earthship Volume I, pages 157 &166) and formed into the wall as it goes up using metal lath masonry ties to anchor the wood frame to the can work. This is similar to the masonry ties tying the columns and beams to can work on the panel wall diagram.

Notice that the cylinder in the section is a double can wall with 6" batt insulation stuffed in the middle. This double wall accommodates the necessary insulation and tension bond beam at the transition point between the cylinder and the hemisphere. It is formed by widening the wall at the top, placing two 1/2" rebar continuous, overlapping 18" at ends and then filling with a concrete mix of 3 parts cement, 4 parts sand, and 5 parts gravel. After construction of the bond beam, the double hemisphere is laid up using the radius gauge as a guide. On double domes, both walls go up simultaneously.

Fifty gallon barrels cut in half or five gallon buckets are laid into the walls just like large cans and used for porthole windows. Do not put them close together. All openings should be kept at least 3'-0" apart. Handmade wooden porthole windows can be attached to the inside of the barrel or bucket. The double dome is closed using a washtub with the bottom cut out or custom made facsimile. This makes a skylight by simply

caulking in a triple pane piece of insulated safety glass before plastering the roof.

The entire dome is plastered with two coats of conventional masonry plaster mix which is usually 1 cement to 3 plaster sand. The plaster mix is applied directly over the can work and should have a waterproof additive such as Anti-hydro put into the mix.

Masonry can domes are serious structures. They require only one skill for walls and roof, but that skill must be **competently** executed. No two cans should ever touch each other in a can dome. The cement between the cans is the real compressive strength of the structure. Consequently, it must be mixed accurately and thoroughly. The aluminum cans simply allow one to lay up a lightweight cement dome without forms. If properly executed, an aluminum can dome can be buried with 2-3 feet of earth. Again, we urge you to experiment with something under 10 feet in diameter before attempting a larger dome.

THE SINGLE BURIED DOME

This dome requires less can work but the excavation expense brings it back up to nearly the same effort as the double dome. It is, however, a unique and simple thermal mass structure. The buried dome is laid by driving a stake in the ground at the desired center of the dome. Put a nail in the top of the stake and tie a cord to it. Make the cord the length of the radius of the plan circle. Tie a little wood handle on the end of the cord and this will make a radius gauge for the entire dome.

The foundations need only be 10" deep and 16" wide because they will be well below the frost line. Two pieces of 1/2" rebar should run continuously in the foundations. The foundations are broken to allow for an arch igloo entrance.

The excavation of the floor (2'-0" to 3'-0") should take place before can laying begins. The excavation can initially be cut with a backhoe but final trim should be done by hand to be sure the footings are not undermined. Plaster this resulting 2-3 foot dirt cliff with two coats of mud formula. (See Earthship Volume I, Chapter 9). Apply one coat with your hands and let dry for two days then apply the second coat.

Cans are laid in a 1 part cement to 3 parts sand mortar mix with 1-1/2" spaces between cans in the lower courses and 1/2" spaces in the upper courses. The radius gauge will guide the arc of the dome in every direction. These single domes are turned up at the top like a turtle neck to receive a skylight. Leave a few cans out at the very top and set 1/2" anchor bolts in a cement pocket. This will provide anchorage for a wood plate to receive a skylight. This wood plate should have metal flashing that extends out to cover the exposed insulation at the top of the dome.

The igloo entrance and the turtle neck for the skylight are both fairly tricky. They require more patience than skill. One course at a time just turn the cans where you want them to go, never allowing them to touch each other. Cans can be tapped into a wedge shape with a hammer to accommodate sharp turns.

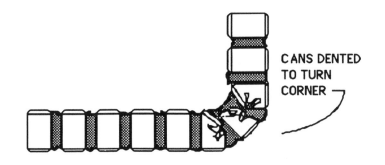

CANS DENTED
TO TURN
CORNER

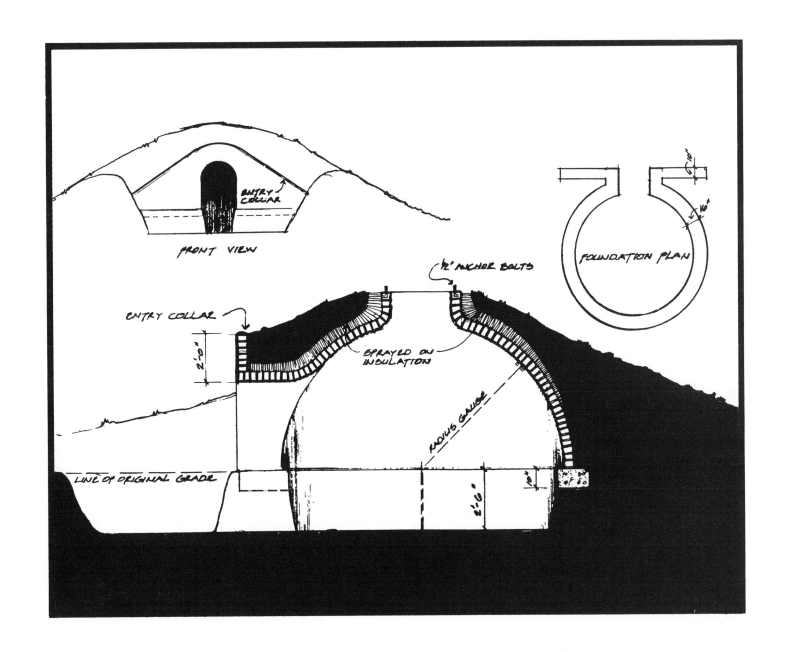

FRONT VIEW

ENTRY COLLAR

FOUNDATION PLAN

½" ANCHOR BOLTS

ENTRY COLLAR

SPRAYED ON INSULATION

RADIUS GAUGE

LINE OF ORIGINAL GRADE

A masonite form could be helpful as a guide on the entrance. A door frame can be anchored to the walls of the entrance by punching out cans and setting anchor bolts and cement in the void. The collar around the igloo entry retains the earth around it.

Before burial, the dome should be sprayed with some type of insulation. Cellulose or urethane are both good for this purpose. Rigid, one inch thick foam insulation has also been "cut and fit" in this situation. Apply a thick layer near the top and taper it to nothing about half way down. At this point the dome is deep enough that no insulation is needed. It should be pointed out that the buried dome would be satisfactory without any insulation in temperate climates. Two coats of plaster with engineering fibers* should be applied before burial. The plaster mix should be 1 part cement to 3 parts plaster sand. It can be applied directly onto the can work and should have a waterproof additive such as Anti-hydro* put into the mix.

*3 and 4 see Appendix, Chapter 11

VAULTS

Vaults, arches and vaulted hallways follow much the same procedures and mortar mixes. Remember to use engineering fibers in all dome or vault mortar mixes. This will definitely make your structure stronger and last longer. Forms are necessary only as a guide or to make it possible to work faster, i.e. more courses in a single day. String or chain gauges without forms will guide you through almost any labirynth of spaces you can imagine. It is important to note that geometric and/or true natural shapes are stronger than organic funky shapes in these applications. For example, vaults should always be made using a cantenary curve. This is the curve a chain would make if you held it upside down. It is a natural shape (egg like) found in nature. Hemispheres and half circles have a thrust that must be contained, hence the necessity for the bond beam described on page 217.

If you want to seriously use the methods described in this chapter for dwelling spaces, we advise that you consult an engineer or Solar Survival Architecture for design of the shapes. The same structural masonry principals of design that have prevailed in arches. domes and vaults through the ages apply here. The only difference is that we are using cans to form the concrete as opposed to bricks between mortar.

226

APPENDIX

Geometric Shapes, Arcs and Curves
Architectural Graphic Standards
by Ramsey and Sleeper
The American Institute of Architects
Publisher - John Wiley and Sons, Inc.

Engineering Fibers
Fibermesh Company
4019 Industry Drive
Chattanooga, TN 37416

Stucco
El Rey
4100 Broadway SE
Albuquerque, NM 87105
(505) 873-1180

Acrylic (Tinted Polymer Based Finish)
El Rey
4100 Broadway SE
Albuquerque, NM 87105
(505) 873-1180

MODERN ECONOMICS

AN OLD MAN AND A SPIDER ONCE MADE A DEAL. THE OLD MAN WANTED A CLOAK AND THE SPIDER WANTED TO TRAVEL. THE OLD MAN WAS TO CARRY THE SPIDER ON A JOURNEY WITH HIM IF THE SPIDER WOULD SPIN THE OLD MAN A CLOAK WHILE HE RODE. NEITHER ONE TRUSTED THE OTHER THAT MUCH. "IF YOU STOP SPINNING, NO MORE RIDING" SAID THE OLD MAN. "IF YOU STOP TRAVELING, NO MORE SPINNING " SAID THE SPIDER. THE OLD MAN BEGAN HIS JOURNEY AND THE SPIDER BEGAN SPINNING. DOWN MANY TRAILS AND ACROSS STREAMS AND THROUGH CITIES THE OLD MAN CARRIED THE SPIDER. ALL THIS TIME THE SPIDER WAS BUSY SPINNING THE CLOAK. THE SPIDER LOVED THE TRAVELING SO HE SPUN MADLY OUT OF FEAR THAT THE OLD MAN WOULD KICK HIM OFF. THE OLD MAN WANTED THE CLOAK MORE AND MORE AS IT BEGAN TO TAKE SHAPE SO HE TRAVELED AND TRAVELED OUT OF FEAR THAT THE SPIDER WOULD STOP SPINNING.. AFTER MANY MILES OF TRAVEL, THE OLD MAN BEGAN TO MOVE SLOWER AND SLOWER AS THE CLOAK WAS GETTING HEAVIER AND HEAVIER. STILL HE TRAVELED NOT REALIZING THE CLOAK WAS BEGINNING TO RESTRICT HIS MOVEMENT. THE SPIDER HAD GROWN TO LOVE THE TRAVELING AND CONVINCED THE OLD MAN THAT MUCH MORE SPINNING HAD TO BE DONE TO PROPERLY FINISH THE CLOAK. AFTER MANY MORE MILES THE OLD MAN COULD HARDLY MOVE BUT HE KEPT TRAVELING AS THE SPIDER, WHO BY NOW WAS ADDICTED TO TRAVEL, KEPT CONVINCING HIM HE NEEDED A BETTER CLOAK. AFTER MANY MORE DAYS OF TRAVEL THE OLD MAN WAS BARELY ABLE TO INCH ALONG, BEING RESTRICTED BY THE THICK HEAVY CLOAK THAT KEPT GETTING THICKER AND MORE CONFINING. THE SPIDER WAS, AT THIS POINT, ABSOLUTELY AFRAID OF ANY OTHER KIND OF LIFE AND, THINKING THAT IF HE STOPPED SPINNING THE OLD MAN WOULD NOT LET HIM RIDE ANY MORE, KEPT SPINNING AND SPINNING. THICKER AND HEAVIER THE CLOAK GOT UNTIL FINALLY IT WAS IMPOSSIBLE FOR THE OLD MAN TO MOVE. HE COULD NO LONGER CONTINUE HIS JOURNEY. HE STOPPED AND ROLLED DOWN ON THE GROUND SMOTHERED BY HIS OWN CLOAK. THE SPIDER WAS STRANDED.

PART THREE
FACTORS OF THE EARTHSHIP

12. LANDSCAPING

F A C T O R S

THE EARTHSHIP IS AS MUCH A PART OF THE
EARTH AS IT IS A **BUILDING**. FOR THIS
REASON EARTHSHIP LANDSCAPING IS AS MUCH
A PART OF THE **BUILDING** AS IT IS A PART OF
THE **EARTH**. LANDSCAPING FOR EARTHSHIPS
IS PART OF THE ROOFING AND DRAINAGE
SYSTEM, PART OF THE CATCHWATER SYSTEM,
PART OF THE GREY WATER SYSTEM, ETC.
THIS, TOGETHER WITH SOME NECESSARY
REGIONAL AND GLOBAL AWARENESS, MAKES
LANDSCAPING AN EARTHSHIP SOMETHING
MORE THAN JUST A DECORATIVE PROJECT. IT
IS A PROJECT THAT CAN ENHANCE AND IN
SOME CASES *MAKE POSSIBLE* THE
PERFORMANCE OF AN EARTHSHIP. IMPROPER
LANDSCAPING CAN, ON THE OTHER HAND,
RENDER AN EARTHSHIP *DEAD IN THE WATER*
SO TO SPEAK. IT IS, THEREFORE, NECESSARY
TO TAKE THE INFORMATION IN THIS CHAPTER
AS SERIOUSLY AS THE EARTHSHIP STRUCTURE
ITSELF.

Landscaping affects many aspects of Earthship design and performance. We will take these aspects one at a time and discuss their interface with landscaping.

EARTHSHIP STRUCTURE

The structure of the Earthship "U" module as presented in Earthsip Volume I is basically created by a "U" shape made of tires rammed with earth thus creating two parallel walls tied together because of the "U" shape. This "U" has tremendous bearing capacity.

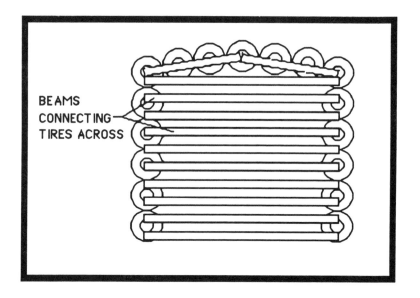

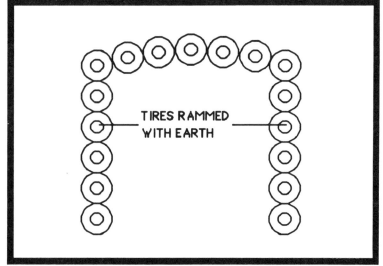

The open end of the "U" is stabilized by the beams connecting the two legs together

The "U" itself and the addition of the beams and decking (which in effect make a diaphragm connecting the two legs of the "U") result in a very rigid, structurally self-contained shape. The only possible movement of this structure would be in the east west direction.

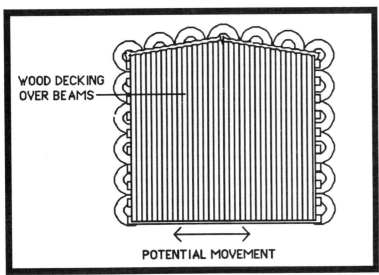

WOOD DECKING
OVER BEAMS

POTENTIAL MOVEMENT

The wing walls of the "U" are designed to eliminate this possibility.

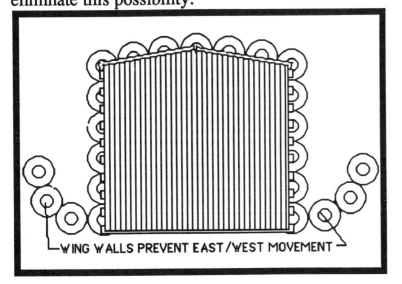

WING WALLS PREVENT EAST/WEST MOVEMENT

Since many Earthships are submerged sometimes as much as five feet, the tire work is not very high and the structure above without burial would be more than adequate.

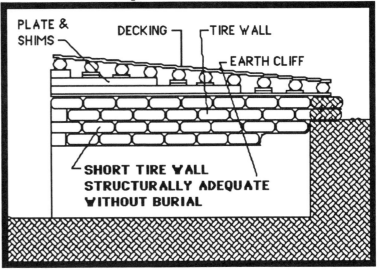

PLATE & SHIMS   DECKING   TIRE WALL

EARTH CLIFF

SHORT TIRE WALL
STRUCTURALLY ADEQUATE
WITHOUT BURIAL

When the building is not submerged much and the tire walls get higher, the added strength and stability of berming earth up against the structure creates a situation where the earth is *against and into* the voids between tires thus rendering the building literally a part of the earth itself.

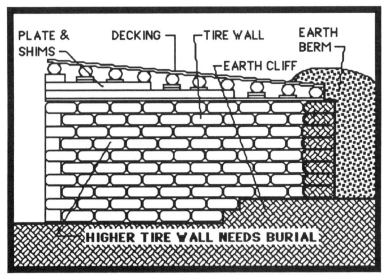

In this case the building is *locked into* the surrounding earth.

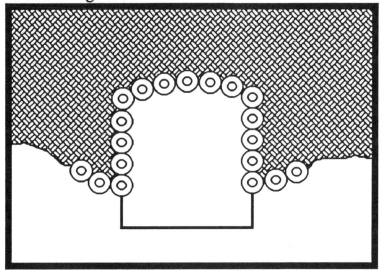

This concept works for one or many "U"s

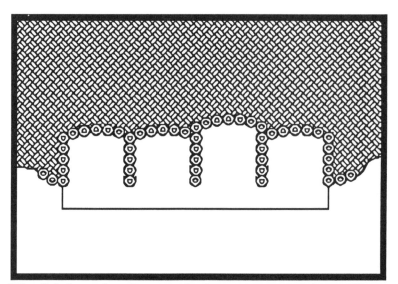

The higher the tire work the more positive effect the burial or "berming" can have as it stabilizes the higher walls by almost becoming a part of them. It should be noted that Earthships can be built with no berming at all but this requires more overall structural analysis not to mention insulation and plaster i.e. more money. When an Earthship is "snuggled" into the earth, it is actually being structurally reinforced by the earth against any structural movement. The walls are no longer free standing walls, they are (because of the voids between the tires) knitted into the surrounding earth. **Thus, berming up earth against an Earthship is a factor of landscaping that has a positive effect on the structure of the building and is advisable if at all possible.**

ROOFING
Conventional housing sets on the earth.

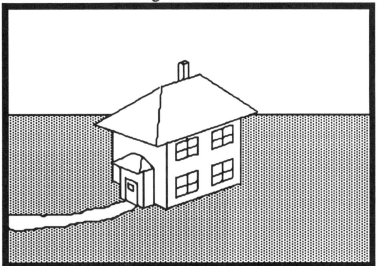

Earthships are in and a part of the earth.

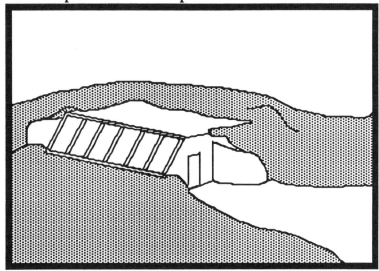

Consequently, when roofing an Earthship one is also roofing the earth as the details in Earthship Volume I illustrate.

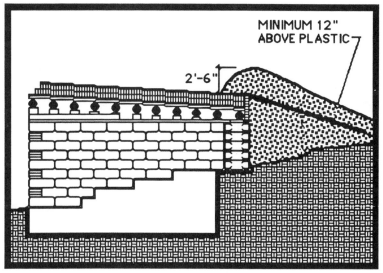

This fact has serious effects on planting near the building. Conventional planting and landscaping techniques are not valid for Earthship landscaping. Conventional housing allows planting of trees or shrubs right against the building.

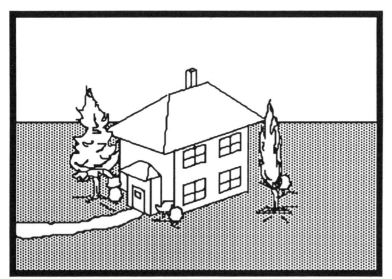

Planting of trees or shrubs near an Earthship would require punching a hole in the "roof".

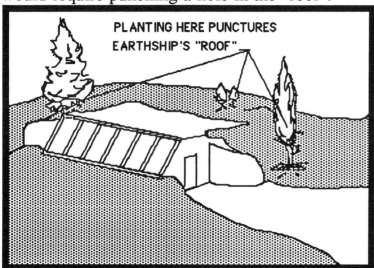

PLANTING HERE PUNCTURES EARTHSHIP'S "ROOF"

This is one of the most common mistakes made by owners of Earthships. Remember, **your berm around your Earthship is also an integral**

part of your roof. Only ground covers such as wild flowers ands grass can be planted here. Trees and plants with deep roots and wells for catching water around them should be kept 20 feet away from the tire walls.

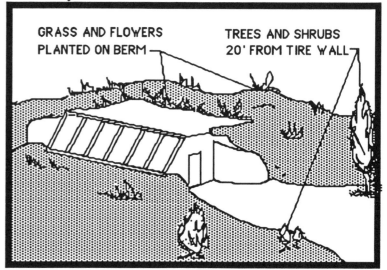

GRASS AND FLOWERS PLANTED ON BERM

TREES AND SHRUBS 20' FROM TIRE WALL

The earth berm, in addition to having structural effects, is also part of the roof. It actually contains roofing material 12" down and creates the slope to carry water (quickly) away from the inner building. The surface water is manipulated up to fifty feet from the building. It is carried away from the walls and off in the direction the site would naturally have it go. Almost every site has a slight slope in one direction. You simply find this slope with a builders level. Shoot a few elevations and run your water from the berm around the Earthship toward the prevailing slope of the site no matter how subtle it is.

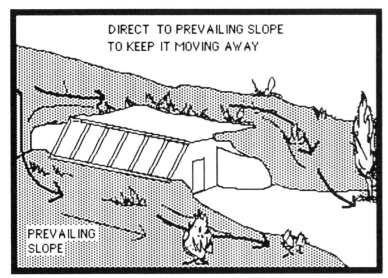

DIRECT TO PREVAILING SLOPE TO KEEP IT MOVING AWAY

PREVAILING SLOPE

MORE PLANTING ON DOWN HILL SIDE OF BUILDING

Do not create any dips, swales or planting conditions that hold water anywhere near the tire walls. Move surface water away from the building fast by sculpting the land. Water can be directed toward landscaping areas (trees and shrubs) a safe distance from the walls of the building. This safe distance varies with the nature of the site. A site with a good slope would allow major tree planting closer to the building on the downhill side of the building.

Flatter sites would require at least twenty feet between the Earthship and trees or anything requiring a deep hole filled with water. Following is a photo of a north entrance into an Earthship with wildflower and ground cover landscaping which does not impede the flow of water <u>away</u> from the buried walls of the building.

237

Another consideration with respect to planting near an Earthship is to plant indigenous plants that will be happy with local rainfall as their only water supply. If you are using a catch water system this is usually a must. The idea here is that **you do not want to be the one adding water to the area around your Earthship and you want to carefully manipulate the water that comes from the sky.** There are exceptions to this with respect to the grey water discussion that follows.

GREY WATER
Some grey water must go to exterior planters. This is the only water recommended to be purposefully placed near an Earthship. The locations for grey water planters are carefully thought out with respect to prevailing slope and proximity to the tire walls. The deeper the building is in the ground the more critical this situation is. Grey water locations should generally follow the same rules presented in the discussion above.

Grey water usually comes out the south (front face) side of the Earthship and this is the least vulnerable area because there is no plastered tire wall here. In most cases there is a planter along this wall that would welcome any dampness that occurred.

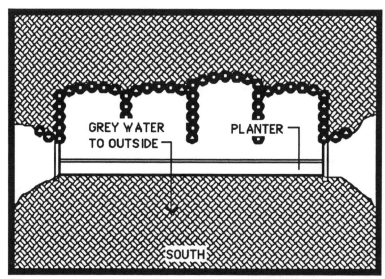

Since most Earthship owners choose a south sloping site, the grey water coming out the south side is running away from the building naturally and there is no potential problem.

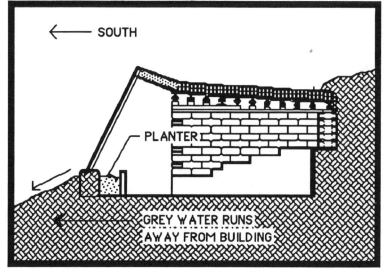

Planting beds can occur as close as desired in this situation. The only factor here would be the effect that tall plants would have on the solar gain of the front face.

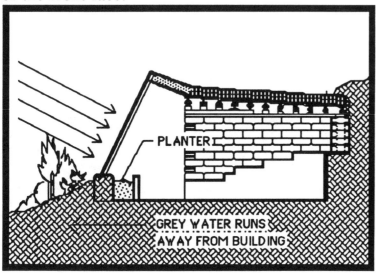

If the site is not sloped to the south, orient the grey water planting toward the prevailing slope and keep it at least twenty feet from the building.

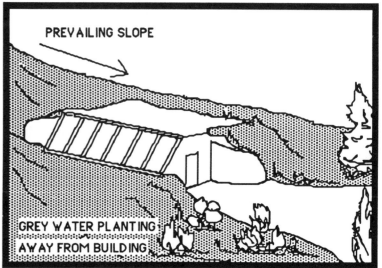

Many Earthships use catchwater systems which don't allow much landscape watering. This makes a grey water planting area the only area with the potential of being watered regularly. Grey water can be irrigated to many little beds or trees or gardens. Grey water is a major factor in Earthship landscaping. Use this wisely and keep it away from the tire walls. Except for the south side, get it away from the building fast and develop your own little jungle.

CATCHWATER
Catchwater life usually does not allow the wasteful decadent use of water that most of us are accustomed to. Catchwater life requires indigenous landscaping capable of survival on local rainfall with grey watered planned planting areas. This is one good reason to save every

existing tree possible - so you don't have to start so many new ones as this takes water. Landscaping an Earthship involves sculpting and shaping the terrain to manipulate the water where you want it - usually away from the building. Now, since you are already sculpting and manipulating water, you may as well take this one step further in your landscaping efforts. You can create uphill swales away from and on the downhill side of your Earthship to catch and retain water so it will soak into the ground rather than just run off quickly.

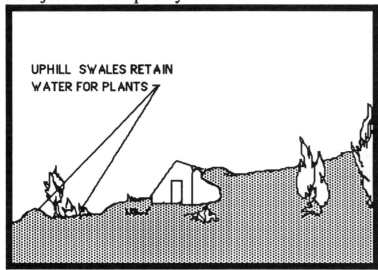

This is just the opposite of what you want to do immediately around your building. These swales trap water and allow it to soak in slowly to provide moisture for plants below. If your Earthship is below, it will provide moisture there too. This, you don't want. We are moving water

quickly away near the building and trapping it in areas safely away from the building. In some cases where roof water is not enough to provide adequate water supply, the land is further sculpted toward a lined tank and stored with the roof water.

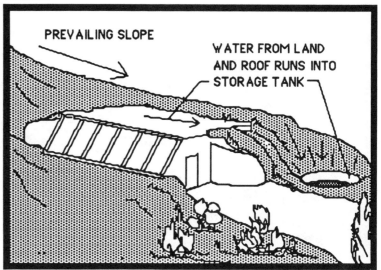

The thing to remember here is that you can move water away fast by surface contours and you can trap it by surface contours. You are the designer and all you have to know is where you want and don't want water, then do it.

INSULATION

Earth is not a very good insulator. However, <u>enough</u> earth does prevent the penetration of cold or heat. For example in areas where the winters reach 30 degrees below zero, the ground does not freeze below 4 feet. Therefore, four feet of earth is enough insulation to maintain temperatures above freezing in this area. This area would have a 4 foot frost line. Earthship landscaping tries to recreate the frost line and make it higher by sculpting and contouring the land.

Berming and burying the parapet of the Earthship actually recreates the frostline as it recreates the surface of the earth. This is another reason to bury and berm against an Earthship. Every wall of an Earthship except the south glass wall should be buried with an earth berm parapet if possible. Many people want to expose various walls of their Earthship to get windows, views and entrances. This adversly effects structure, water-proofing and insulation (and price$$) all at once.

The discussions above illustrate how seriously landscaping is related to the overall performance of an Earthship. The most often repeated mistake is to turn the landscaping over to someone unfamiliar with the principals of Earthship design. They can cause one catastrophe after another. Landscaping is as important to the Earthship owner as manipulating sails is to the sailor. Not many sailors turn this job over to anyone.

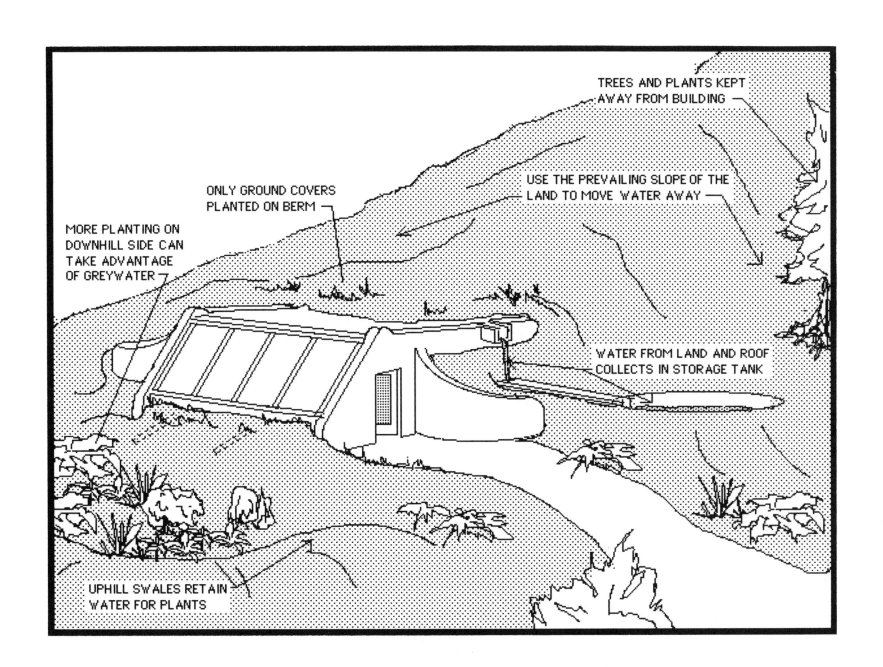

TREES AND PLANTS KEPT AWAY FROM BUILDING

USE THE PREVAILING SLOPE OF THE LAND TO MOVE WATER AWAY

ONLY GROUND COVERS PLANTED ON BERM

MORE PLANTING ON DOWNHILL SIDE CAN TAKE ADVANTAGE OF GREYWATER

WATER FROM LAND AND ROOF COLLECTS IN STORAGE TANK

UPHILL SWALES RETAIN WATER FOR PLANTS

243

244

13 CODES, PERMITS & FINANCING
F   A   C   T   O   R   S

BUILDING CODES AND LENDING INSTITUTIONS BASICALLY CONTROL THE TYPE OF HOUSING THAT IS AVAILABLE OR POSSIBLE. THIS IS BECAUSE BUILDING PERMITS AND FINANCING MUST BE OBTAINED PRIOR TO BUILDING. MOST NEW OR DIFFERENT CONCEPTS HAVE TO BE RIGOROUSLY PROVEN TO THE BUILDING CODE OFFICIALS AS OFFICIALS ARE NOT BEING PAID TO TAKE RISKS ON NEW IDEAS. THEY ARE BEING PAID TO ENFORCE EXISTING DOGMA. CONSEQUENTLY, THEY TEND TO GO BY THE EXISTING BOOKS REGARDLESS OF ENVIRONMENTAL OR HUMAN ISSUES TO MAKE SURE THEY DON'T LOSE THEIR JOBS. TO FURTHER COMPLICATE THE MATTER, THE LENDING INSTITUTIONS DO NOT NECESSARILY ACCEPT ANY APPROVALS OF NEW IDEAS BY THE BUILDING CODE OFFICIALS ANYWAY. THEIR OBJECTIVE IS TO SECURE THE RESALE VALUE OF THE DWELLING TO COVER THEMSELVES IN CASE OF DEFAULT BY THE BORROWER. CONSEQUENTLY THEY STICK TO THINGS THAT HAVE PROVEN TO RE-SELL OVER THE YEARS REGARDLESS OF WHETHER THEY ARE APPROPRIATE FOR THE PLANET OR FOR PEOPLE. WHAT WE HAVE FACING US IS A FORMIDABLE MOUNTAIN RANGE OF OBSOLETE DOGMA INHABITED BY BUILDING CODE OFFICIALS AND LOAN OFFICERS WHO ARE FROM A DIFFERENT WORLD THAN THOSE OF US WANTING TO BUILD AND SAIL IN EARTHSHIPS. THIS CHAPTER DISCUSSES THE ART OF DEALING WITH THOSE INDIVIDUALS AND ULTIMATELY CROSSING THE MOUNTAIN RANGE TO THE "PROMISED LAND".

I WISH TO POINT OUT THAT I HAVE WORKED WITH THE NEW MEXICO CONSTRUCTION INDUSTRIES DIVISION FOR TWENTY YEARS IN DEVELOPING THE EARTHSHIP CONCEPT. THEY ARE AN EXCEPTION TO THE GENERAL NATURE OF BUILDING CODE OFFICIALS. THEY HAVE BOTH ALLOWED AND SEEN THE VALUE IN THE EVOLUTION OF THE EARTHSHIP. THEY HAVE CHALLENGED THE WEAK POINTS AND ENCOURAGED THE STRONG POINTS OF THE EARTHSHIP CONCEPT. THE NEW MEXICO C.I.D. IS AN EXAMPLE FOR OTHER STATES TO FOLLOW.

I once had a banana plant in my office. It was on the back north wall of a solar space - a prototype of an Earthship.

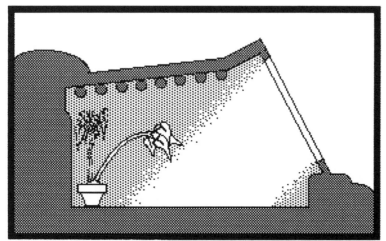

When I first placed it there it stood straight up. SLOWLY OVER TIME, I NOTICED IT LEANING TOWARD THE LIGHT COMING FROM THE SOUTH SOLAR FACE. AFTER A FEW MONTHS IT WAS LEANING SO MUCH IT WAS ABOUT TO FALL OVER. THE STALK OF THE PLANT IS QUITE RIGID. IF I TRIED TO BEND IT IN AN INSTANT FROM ITS STRAIGHT UP POSITION TO ITS NOW LEANING POSITION IT WOULD HAVE BROKEN. HOWEVER, THE SLOW INCH BY INCH LEANING THAT IT DID ON ITS OWN EVERY DAY ALLOWED IT TO MAKE A RADICAL CHANGE IN ITS POSITION OVER TIME. THE POINT HERE IS THAT RADICAL CHANGE OR *FLEXIBILITY* IS A

FUNCTION OF TIME. IMMEDIATE RADICAL CHANGE WOULD HAVE BROKEN THE PLANT. THE SAME IS TRUE OF BUILDING CODES AND LENDING INSTITUTIONS. WE MUST BE AWARE OF THE FACT THAT THEY ARE NOT CAPABLE OF RADICAL OVERNIGHT CHANGE. THEY WILL BREAK OR BREAK US. WE MUST ALLOW THEM TO LEAN A LITTLE MORE EVERY DAY TOWARD THE CONCEPT OF EARTHSHIPS. THE LEAN HAPPENED TO THE BANANA PLANT IN SMALL DOSES - THE EARTHSHIP MUST BE PRESENTED TO THE POWERS THAT BE IN SMALL DOSES. *

THE EASY WAY OUT

Since the Earthship does not need electricity, well water or sewers for construction or operation, remote land (which is far less expensive) is always an option. Remote land always has fewer restrictions than land right in a subdivision. Building officials always tend to be more adamant about the letter of the code in highly visible areas such as existing subdivisions, "developed estates", etc. The bottom line here is that if you choose remote land (which the Earthship concept allows) you will have an easier time with building officials. In some cases, you won't encounter them at all.

*For more on "The Art of Leaning" see A COMING OF WIZARDS, Chapter 6, by Michael Reynolds.

Since the Earthship is designed for the owner/ builder, slow "out of pocket" construction of the dwelling is possible even for the novice builder. This has already happened in many cases. Of course, you don't start with a ten thousand square foot home. To assure your own success in getting sheltered in a reasonable amount of time with "out of pocket" funding you must start with one or two "U"s, get them livable, then add on as you can.

So it stands that our first choice on how to deal with codes and bank loans is to not encounter them at all.

CHOOSE REMOTE LAND
BUILD YOUR OWN EARTHSHIP

BUILDING CODES
WHERE

If you must deal with building code officials on any level there are some pathways to follow. Remember, they will be easier to deal with in less visible locations. Avoid planned subdivisions whenever possible.

Every state follows the same Uniform Building Code. This code has a clause that allows for alternative methods "not covered in this document". It states that alternative methods must meet requirements and standards of those presented in the UBC. Your objective would,

therefore, be to illustrate that Earthship construction meets and exceeds the standards put forth in the UBC. In New Mexico, this has already been done. If you plan to build in New Mexico you are home free as far as the codes and permits go.

Every state has a different policy on how approvals are handled. For example, New Mexico has a statewide policy. If something is approved by the state office it holds true all over the state. Colorado (where many Earthships have been built) has a county by county policy which means that each county has the power to interpret alternative methods as they see fit. This means that if one county approves, it does not necessarily mean that the next one will. Several counties in Colorado have approved of this concept. No one has rejected it as of this date. Some, however, have been more difficult than others to deal with. Thus the first step is to find how your state operates and then you will know where to go to present the concept.

HOW
Step One - Presenting the Concept

If your particular state or county has not already approved an Earthship, you must first present the concept. Solar Survival Press has documents and videos that will help with this. The following items will help in initially presenting the concept to an official:

ENGINEERING REPORT - a twenty page document analyzing the structural integrity of tire walls as used in the Dennis Weaver Home in Ridgway Colorado. This document shows experiments, graphs, calculations, photographs, and conclusions which support the structural concept entirely. It was put together by a licensed engineer in Colorado.

DENNIS WEAVER VIDEO - a 30 minute color video going from the ground up on Dennis Weavers home in Colorado. It contains interviews with building inspectors, congressmen, engineers and the architect. This is a very professional video financed and executed by Dennis Weaver himself. It contains explicit graphics and structural footage.

HOW-TO VIDEO - a 30 minute color video explicitly focusing on the tire and can techniques - how to execute them and why they work.

EARTHSHIP VOLUME I - The "how - to" that presents the Earthship concept. This book is packed with evey kind of information about the concept. You can't expect a building official to read it cover to cover but skimming through it will help give the concept credibility.

Presenting the above items will introduce your building officials to the concept. This information is well presented and to the point. 95% of the time you will get a favorable reception to the concept from this information. This is all you are looking for at this point.

Step Two - Presenting Your Project

Now you must evaluate the reception that you got to your initial presentation of the concept. You determine the scope of your initial project based on this reception. If it was overwhelmingly good, you could present a reasonable sized simple "by the book Earthship" as your project that you are requesting a permit for. If the reception was somewhat skeptical then you reduce the scope of what you are asking for. The point is to not ask for too much at first. Under the worst circumstances, you may only want to ask for a demonstration permit for one "U". A demonstration permit is simply for demonstration. You do not present it as your home. You say you will use it only if they approve of it after physical observation. You may think this is risky. However, when a building inspector walks in a finished "U" in early February, feels how warm it is with no heating system and experiences the structure himself, you will have no problem in getting him to allow you to occupy it. What you are doing here is allowing an official the chance to see the concept before he is asked to risk his job on it. You are asking small inch by inch steps (like the banana tree) of him. Rarely would a building official refuse a demonstration. This puts the risk on your shoulders not his. Officials, engineers and even skeptics have always been impressed upon actual on site observation of an Earthship "U".

The point here is to determine just how small of a"bite" to ask the inspector to swallow in this phase. It is better to have it too small that too large both for you and the inspector. One or two "U"s is a good demonstration size and can easily be evolved into phase one of your total home.

You present this demonstration as a <u>rammed earth</u> thermal mass dwelling - not a rubber tire house. Rammed earth is a term that many are familiar with. Earthships are in fact rammed earth. The earth is rammed in steel belted casings. This makes a rammed earth brick more durable than conventional rammed earth or adobe. Another factor of your presentation is not to mention all the other systems at first. Get approval on the structural concept of the Earthship first, then go for the systems. If you go to a building inspector and say I want build a rubber tire house with grey water, catch water, compost toilets and solar electric systems, he will definitely freak. That is just too much new stuff to lay on him all at once. You go and present the concept - get a feeling for

his reception to that and then ask to build a small demonstration unit or prototype to illustrate the concept - that is all. You design this demonstration to be *phase one* of your total project. After you have structural approval, you begin with the systems.

As with the Earthship itself, your various systems will meet with less and less resistance the more remote you are.

SOLAR ELECTRICAL SYSTEM
As presented in chapter one, your Earthship will be absolutely conventionally wired. You will therefore need no special approval for solar electricity. The systems presented in chapter one are already approved by electric codes. You should have no trouble with solar electric approval if you even have to mention it.

CATCH WATER SYSTEM
The catch water system requires nothing out of the ordinary from the conventional pressure tank on. The source of your water (whether well or stream or spring or city) is not a thing that has to be approved. In terms of running water your "in-house system" is conventional and needs no approval. The catch water systems presented in chapter two use totally conventional in-house plumbing. As above, I would not even mention catch water because it doesn't effect your house

249

plumbing.

GREY WATER SYSTEMS

There are counties in California that have approved and advocate the use of grey water systems. This is due to existing water shortages. In view of this and the potential future water shortages in many parts of the USA, grey water systems are being allowed in many areas. Here, the best thing to do, after you have received approval to build the Earthship itself, is to present the information in chapter three to your official. They may allow it but will still make you install vents and traps. This is a small price to pay. Some areas will make you put all grey water in a tank and pump it out for later use. Some areas will not allow it at the present time. In these instances you can fight (and we will help you if possible) or you can do it the way they want but including certain fittings in certain places to allow you to valve the water where you want to yourself after the final inspection.

COMPOST TOILETS

There are places that do not allow compost toilets. This is mainly because some of the early ones were pretty bad. Presenting the new technology and possibly a demonstration to your official is the best way here. Again, do not attempt this until you have approval for your Earthship itself. The new SUNMAR compost toilets presented in chapter three actually flush and should meet approval almost everywhere. If you have trouble, contact SSA OR SUNMAR for assistance.

Remember, all these systems are minor battles compared to the approval of your Earthship itself. Do not cloud the issue (or scare your inspector) by attempting to get these approved at the same time. The plumbing is the only possible disapproval you may have on these systems and plumbing is not dealt with in an Earthship until the structure is up. After your inspector has seen that the Earthship is a very positive approach to building, you can explore the possibilities of the slightly unconventional plumbing necessary for grey water and compost toilets.

FINANCING

This is a difficult area for me because I view the savings and loan associations of the USA as neck and neck with nuclear power plants in terms of harm to the country. There is no right way to use a nuclear power plant. Likewise, there is no right way to use a savings and loan mortgage. They are a rip off. They have been managed and developed by dishonest people and everyone today (early 1990's) is aware of the condition of the S&Ls relative to mismanagement and greed. They sell the use of money at a very high price and they hold all the cards. They even control the type of house you build. My best advice is to avoid them if at all possible.

One method of avoiding them is to build slowly out of pocket. The Earthship concept does allow this and I have seen it work for many people. Obviously, there are those for whom this will not work. The next best thing is to get small business type bank loan that doesn't involve the project at hand. Another possibility is to get a second mortgage or home equity loan on your existing home. The bottom line is to try to get money any other way than an S&L loan. If these avenues don't work then you can try an S&L loan. Begin this process about one year before you want the money and use the same approach as you used on the building code officials. Be prepared to make some compromises (or deceptions) and be prepared to pay. S&Ls have loaned money on Earthships. We have had to install phony back up electric baseboard heaters to satisfy them as well as a few other ridiculous things that make them happy. Remember, present it as rammed earth and do not mention the rest of the systems at first.

There is a lending institution that has loaned and says they will continue to loan on Earthships. They have affiliates all over the country. The company name is Stanchart Mortgage Company, 3200 N Central, Albuquerque, NM. The contact name and phone number is Ray Mendoza, (505) 883-6213.

They will have certain requirements that will slightly affect your design or systems and will require a complete set of construction drawings (see last page of book). They will also require the stamp of an architect and an engineer on your construction drawings. All of this is possible, it simply involves more time and money just to get started.

It will be much easier to acquire your loan if you have a large down payment relative to the proposed cost of your Earthship. Normally, lending institutions only loan 60% to 80% of the proposed price of the project. If you have more than 20% as a down payment, it will look much better for you.

Another requirement you can expect is the use of a licensed contractor to build the project. This will obviously add 15% to 20% to the cost of the project for his fee, unless you can make a deal with him to just be the "figure head" and let you build it. You might even need him for some conventional construction advice. Using a licensed contractor for a "figure head" and consultant involves a much smaller fee and is often the best way to go. If you do have a contractor build your Earthship, you should have him attend a Solar Survival Seminar on how to build Earthships (see last page of this book).

EPILOGUE

The information presented in Earthship Vol I and Earthship Vol II is not the final word. It is the beginning of a journey. In a world where a healthy economy has become more important than a healthy planet and healthy people, we have found that it is time to leave the place where we are. When you are in a burning building and you see a way out, you don't sit down and decide where you are going. You take the way out and survive, then you are in a position to think about where to go. This is the purpose of the EARTHSHIP concept. It is a way out of the "fire" of modern civilization. There are definite improvements and evolutions of various aspects of the concept that are and will be developing, however **the "boat" floats now.**

We have developed a small prototype community called **REACH - R**ural **E**arthship **A**lternative **C**ommunity **H**abitat. This is a community of EARTHSHIPS that is **being built** with the same solar power systems that are going to provide electricity for living.. It is also **being built** with the same catch water systems that are going to provide water for living. There is no sewage system that dumps into nearby streams as all the buildings deal with their own waste individually via grey water and compost toilet systems. There

is no actual "sale for profit" of land. This community is emerging free of all centralized systems that support conventional housing and feed the economic dinosaur that carries us as it consumes us.

The process of construction uses much more power and water than simply living. If we can *build* with these systems, we can certainly *live* with them. Most housing developments spend hundreds of thousands of dollars on infrastructure (sewage, water, gas and power systems to the houses) before the housing can even begin. Land has to be sold at a tremendous profit to finance this (as well as to make the developers a fortune). The **REACH** project broke ground on the first EARTHSHIP the very day we closed the deal on the land. We needed no infrastructure, no power lines, no wells, no sewers as the EARTHSHIP itself *is* its own infrastructure. The last few months of working on this project have shown us that the "boat" really does float and it will take us anywhere on Earth without leaving a trail of devastation behind. We/you can build EARTHSHIPS and/or communities anywhere you can drive a four wheel drive truck. This opens up some of the most beautiful places on the planet where land is not "valuable" because there is no power or water. We don't need power and water because we get them free from the sky. The journey has begun.

Currently, it is the dependency on centralized conventional utility systems that keeps us from journeying further with our housing. This same kind of "systems dependency" also keeps us from journeying further with our thinking. We have become stationary creatures with regard to our concept of living. This is very dangerous because the unarguable world around us is constantly evolving. We must be mobile enough both mentally and physically to evolve with it. The EARTHSHIP concept provides this mobility physically. That is the beginning of the journey. Mental, emotional and spiritual evolution follows once we are in a physical position to allow it. Our current "stressed out" method of living based on a **hollow economic Wizard of Oz** keeps us running for the dollar. The dollar is just a piece of paper.

The EARTHSHIP concept is meant to place shelter and a less stressful method of living within the immediate grasp of people. If land is made available for no profit; if shelter can be obtained with little or no mortgage payment; if utilities come free from the sky; if much of our food can be grown in our homes; people will become more mobile with their thinking. They will begin to

have time to think of each other and the planet. Peace on Earth will no longer be a dream, it will simply be a result of the way we live.

Michael E. Reynolds

Other books by MICHAEL REYNOLDS

Earthship Volume I, Solar Survival Press
A Coming of Wizards, High Mesa Press

Both available from Solar Survival Architecture

The objective of the Earthship books is to make the concepts we have developed over the years available to people who want an alternative to what we call "living" today on this planet. These concepts have been presented in a very simplified manner. In some cases, more information and/or consultation will be needed by the readers. SSA has many services available to fulfill this need. These services range from full architectural service to architectural consultation and guidance to hands-on seminars throughout the spring, summer and fall of 1992. Due to the numbers of people wanting further Earthship information, all consultation and guidance must be by phone appointment and seminar applicants must make reservations as far in advance as possible. Generic construction drawings are also available for acquiring building permits. These drawings work with any generic floor plans from one to four bedrooms. Owner customized floor plans will also work with these generic plans if generic Earthship concepts are followed.

The information presented in Earthship Volumes I and II has been recently developed and will obviously evolve over the coming months and years. Let us know if you are interested in a newsletter to keep you updated on Earthship evolutions.

SSA is also developing whole communities of Earthships which will offer finished and partly finished Earthships for sale, rent, or lease, as well as guidance programs for building your own Earthship and land parcels for building on. Land in these communities is not sold. Building sites are made available on a membership basis. Write to us for a packet of information on one of the Earthship communities. These information packets will include site surveys, explanations on the structure of the communities, membership fees, objectives, photographs, legal documents for membership association, etc. They will cost $10.

As with any other "build your own" concepts, the execution of the ideas in this book is subject to your own level of competence. These methods have been successful for SSA and show promise of evolving even further. We wish you luck in using them and thank you for your interest in them, however, we cannot be responsible for any applications of any methods put forth in this book unless they are executed under the direct supervision of Solar Survival Architecture.